Passports

William K. Durr
Jean M. LePere
Ruth Hayek Brown

CONSULTANT   Paul McKee

HOUGHTON MIFFLIN COMPANY • Boston

Atlanta • Dallas • Geneva, Illinois • Hopewell, New Jersey • Palo Alto • Toronto

Acknowledgments

For each of the selections listed below, grateful acknowledgment is made for permission to adapt and/or reprint copyrighted material, as follows:

"All Except Sammy." Text copyright © 1966 by Gladys Yessayan Cretan. From *All Except Sammy* by Gladys Yessayan Cretan, by permission of Little, Brown and Company in association with The Atlantic Monthly Press.

"Annie and the Old One." Copyright © 1971 by Miska Miles. From *Annie and the Old One* by Miska Miles, by permission of Little, Brown and Company in association with The Atlantic Monthly Press.

"Autumn Thought." From *The Dream Keeper* by Langston Hughes. Copyright 1932 by Alfred A. Knopf, Inc., and renewed 1960 by Langston Hughes. Reprinted by permission of the publisher.

"Beauty." Reprinted by permission of William Morrow & Co., Inc., from *I Am a Pueblo Indian Girl* by E-Yeh-Shure'. Copyright 1939 by William Morrow & Company, Inc. Copyright renewed 1967 by Louise Abeita Chiwiwi.

"Beware, My Child." Copyright © Shel Silverstein. Reprinted by permission of the author.

"Brother," from *Hello and Goodbye* by Mary Ann Hoberman, published in 1959 by Little, Brown and Company. Reprinted by permission of Russell & Volkening, Inc., as agents for the author. Copyright © 1959 by Mary Ann Hoberman.

"The Case of the Mysterious Tramp," from *Encyclopedia Brown Finds the Clues* by Donald J. Sobol. Reprinted by permission of Thomas Nelson Inc. Copyright © 1966 by Donald J. Sobol.

"Coplas." Reprinted by permission of Four Winds Press, a division of Scholastic Magazines, Inc., from *Coplas, Folk Poems in Spanish and English*, text copyright © 1972 by Toby Talbot.

"Dance of the Animals." From *The Tiger and the Rabbit and Other Tales* by Pura Belpré. Copyright © 1965, 1946, 1944 by Pura Belpré. Reprinted by permission of J. B. Lippincott Company.

"Dr. Penny, Veterinarian." *What Can She Be? A Veterinarian,* by Gloria and Esther Goldreich. Adapted by permission of Lothrop, Lee & Shepard Co., Inc. Copyright © 1972 by Esther and Gloria Goldreich. Reprinted by permission of John Schaffner, Literary Agent. Copyright © 1972 by Gloria and Esther Goldreich and by Robert Ipcar.

"Easy Diver," from *Street Poems* by Robert Froman. Copyright © 1971 by Robert Froman. Reprinted by permission of the publishers, Saturday Review Press/E.P. Dutton & Co., Inc. Reprinted by permission of Curtis Brown, Ltd. Copyright © 1971 by Robert Froman.

"His Majesty the Peasant," by Sally Werner. Reprinted by permission of *Jack and Jill* Magazine, © 1958 The Curtis Publishing Company.

"Inspector Peckit." Slightly adapted from *Inspector Peckit*, Story and Pictures by Don Freeman. Copyright © 1972 by Don Freeman. All rights reserved. Reprinted by permission of The Viking Press, Inc. British rights granted by World's Work Ltd.

"Lewis Has a Trumpet," from *In the Middle of the Trees* by Karla Kuskin. Reprinted by permission of Harper & Row, Publishers, Inc.

"The Lion," by Dusan Radovic. From *The UNICEF Book of Children's Poems*, compiled by William K. Kaufman; adapted for English-reading children by Joan Gilbert Van Poznac. © 1970 by Stackpole Books. Used by permission.

"The Magic Pumpkin." Copyright © 1971 by

Contents

Cavalcade

Safari

Safari

STORIES

POEMS

INFORMATIONAL ARTICLE

SKILL LESSONS

PLAY

The Magic Tree

by GERALD McDERMOTT

Time was, there lived two brothers, Luemba and Mavungu.

Born as twins, they grew and came to be very different.

Their mother loved Luemba. She smiled on him always. She gave him fruit. Mavungu was given nothing.

One night he left his home.

Mavungu came to a place in the river. A great tree was there, so thick he could not pass.

When he pulled the leaves, strange voices spoke to him.

Mavungu was astonished.

From each leaf, a new person.

Last to come was a beautiful girl, a princess.

She thanked Mavungu for releasing her people from The Magic Tree. She vowed that she would take care of him. She touched a charm around her neck. "I want to be his wife, but he is so homely." Again she touched the charm. "I want to be his wife, but he is in rags."

Mavungu was joyful now, joyful and strong.

After a time, they passed near a wide place by the river. The princess made a magnificent village grow up there.

Mavungu married the princess. They exchanged vows of love. But she pledged him to silence:

The source of his wealth and pleasure must always be hidden. The secret of The Magic Tree must never be told.

The sun crossed the sky many times. The moon grew to fullness. And Mavungu thought of his family.

He sent for his mother and his brother. When they came, he treated them kindly.

But his mother wanted to know Mavungu's secret.

He began to tell of his journey down the river. The princess stared at him. His words became as silence.

The sun crossed the sky many times again. Once more the moon grew to fullness. Mavungu could not forget his family.

Alone, he returned to his mother's home.

"Mavungu," said his mother. "You left me long ago. Tell me of your new life."

Mavungu forgot his pledge of silence. He forgot those who loved him. And he gave his secret to those who did not love him at all.

"When I ran away, I found a canoe in the river.
I travelled down the river until I came to a large
tree. I pulled the leaves of the tree and each leaf
became a person. I wed the princess of The
Magic Tree and she made a magnificent village.
I have been very happy there.

The Magic Tree was first an award-winning animated film designed by Gerald McDermott. Then the artist adapted his film into a picture book which was chosen as an Honor Book in the Boston Globe-Horn Book Awards.

Gerald McDermott grew up in Detroit, Michigan. At Cass Technical High School he won a national art competition scholarship to Pratt Institute, a famous art school in New York. Upon graduation, he began to produce and direct a series of films done in his unique style of animation.

Mr. McDermott and his artist wife, Beverly Brodsky McDermott, spent several years in the South of France and now live in the Hudson River Valley, New York. In addition to creating films and writing books, Mr. McDermott is at work on an edition of original silk-screen prints. Other books by Gerald McDermott are *Arrow to the Sun*, *Anansi the Spider*, and *The Stonecutter*.

TRULY MY OWN

I think if I searched a thousand lands
and twice the number in rainbows,
I'd never find one human being
who chose the things that I chose
a person who wanted the things I wanted
or sought what I sought to be

I'd never find one human being
like or comparison to me
and if I traveled seven seas
I still would be alone
for there is no one who thinks like me
for my dreams are truly my own.

—VANESSA HOWARD
age 13

A Visit to the Mayor

by Nellie Burchardt

Betsy and her friend Ellen were worried. They had found a stray cat in the City Housing Project. The cat was about to have kittens, and the weather was getting cold outside. Betsy wanted very much to take the cat as her pet. But there was a rule against keeping pets in the Project.

As they walked up the hill to the store, Betsy suddenly exclaimed, "I've got it!"

"What've you got?" asked Ellen.

"How we can get the Project people to change the rule about pets."

"How?"

"Remember last month your mother and my mother were getting people to sign a petition for more crossing guards on the street? Why couldn't we get up a petition about pets and ask everyone in the Project to sign it?"

"Who would we give it to?" asked Ellen.

"The mayor. I saw a picture of him in the paper yesterday with his dog. If he can have a pet, how come we can't?"

Ellen looked thoughtful. "Do you really think it would work?"

"I don't know, but it's worth trying," said Betsy. "Can you think of any better way to get the rule changed?"

"No."

"Then let's write out the petition as soon as we get back. We can make enough copies for the other kids, and they can help us take them around to all the buildings," said Betsy.

Getting the Signatures

The petition drew smiles and wishes of good luck from most of the people the children asked to sign it. When Betsy rang the first few doorbells, her hands were cold with nervousness. The paper shook when she held it out to be signed. But most of the tenants seemed friendly, and soon she felt at ease.

The old man who answered her next bell could not find his glasses, so Betsy had to read the petition out loud to him. Part of the request had been copied from her mother's petition.

"Mr. Mayor," Betsy read from the paper. "We, the undersigned tenants of the City Housing Project, do respectfully request that the rule against pets in the City Housing Project be changed. Is it fair, Mr. Mayor, for you to have a dog when we are not allowed to have pets of any kind in the Project?"

The old man smiled.

"You're absolutely right, girls," the old man said. "I've often wished I could have a cat myself. And I'll tell you a secret. There's a stray cat down in the bushes that somebody has been feeding." His eyes twinkled.

Betsy and Ellen looked at each other. Ellen burst into giggles. "We're the ones!" she shrieked.

"So that's it!" said the man. "I thought she was looking a lot better lately. Well, of course I'll have to sign your petition then." He signed his name at the end of the list. "How many signatures do you have now?"

"With yours, that makes eighty-seven. But our friends are getting signatures, too."

They had all agreed to meet at Betsy's apartment just before supper. When they counted up all the signatures, they found that they had four hundred and nineteen.

"That ought to be enough," said Betsy. "Tomorrow, right after school, we can take the petition to City Hall."

When word got around that they were going to the Mayor's office, almost all the children who had ever watched the cat being fed turned up at Betsy's apartment. She was stunned at the size of the group.

"Well," she said. "I guess the more we have, the more impressed the mayor will be."

"Now let's all be quiet," said Betsy when they arrived at City Hall. "They'll never let us see the mayor if we make a lot of noise."

The children climbed the steps of the huge stone building. Down the long marble hallway to the mayor's office they walked. The sound of their footsteps was lost in the great, high-ceilinged hall.

As they approached the mayor's office, the other children held back more and more, leaving Betsy in front.

"Excuse me, please," she said to the man at the desk by the door that said MAYOR. "We'd like to see the mayor."

"Do you have an appointment?" asked the man, looking up from his desk.

"No. We didn't know you had to. But we have a petition for him."

The man held out his hand. "I'll take care of it. You needn't wait," he said.

The children looked at each other doubtfully. Ellen shook her head at Betsy but didn't say anything.

"No," said Betsy. "We want to see the mayor
in person."

"I'm sorry, but the mayor is very busy at a
City Council meeting."

The children eyed each other again.

"We'll wait," said Betsy.

"I said the mayor is very busy right now," said
the man, beginning to sound annoyed.

"Oh, that's all right. We have lots of time,"
said Betsy. "We'll sit down and wait till he's
not busy." She turned and led the way to a
bench against the wall. The other children followed her and sat down in a row on the bench.

The man at the desk pushed back his chair and stood up. "Now, listen here, all of you," he said. "I told you that you *can't* wait. The mayor is too busy to have a bunch of noisy kids hanging around the office."

The man seemed quite angry. Betsy wished the other children would not leave all the talking to her.

"But we'll be very quiet. Please — we just *have* to see him," she pleaded. "It's very important."

She started to get up, but hesitated when she saw a door open behind the man's back. A tall, rather stout man stood in the doorway. In the room behind him, Betsy could see people walking around, talking to each other.

The man at the desk did not see the other man. He walked toward the children with his arm raised, pointing at the door down the hall where they had come in.

"I said NO! I'm sorry, but you really must leave," he said.

"Come, come, Mr. Witherspoon," said the tall man. "That's no way to treat a group of future voters."

Mr. Witherspoon turned around. "Oh — Mr. Mayor!" he gasped. "I didn't realize you were there. I'm so sorry if we disturbed you. I — I — I was just trying to persuade these children to leave, but they absolutely refuse to."

"Have you tried twisting their arms?" asked the mayor, with a wink at the children.

"Twisting their arms!" exclaimed Mr. Witherspoon in a horrified voice. Then he laughed when he realized the mayor was joking.

"But I'm glad you didn't persuade them to leave," continued the mayor. "It's not every day that I get a chance to talk to a group of my younger constituents."

The children exchanged puzzled looks.

"Now don't tell me that you didn't know you were my constituents," said the mayor with a smile.

The children shook their heads.

"Well, don't let it worry you. It just means you're the people I represent. You know what that means, don't you?"

The children nodded their heads.

"Now," said the mayor. "Out with it. To what do I owe the honor of this visit?"

Betsy Explains

Ellen gave Betsy a shove, and Betsy had to take a step forward to keep her balance.

"Yes?" said the mayor.

When he looked at her, her stomach felt shaky. He had not seemed so enormous in the picture she had seen in the paper.

"We—we—we have a petition here for you, M—Mr. Mayor," stuttered Betsy. She was surprised to hear how little and shaky her voice sounded. She handed him the papers covered with signatures.

The mayor took the papers from Betsy with one hand, and with the other he reached into his pocket and pulled out his glasses. He adjusted them on his nose and read the petition. Then he turned the pages of signatures one by one and examined them carefully.

Finally he looked up at Betsy and said, "So I can have a pet and you can't, is that it?"

"Yes, sir," said Betsy in a tiny voice.

"And you don't think that's fair, eh?"

"N—n—no, sir."

"What kind of pet would you get if you could have one?" asked the mayor.

Betsy took a deep breath. "A cat. You see, there's this poor little cat that has a lame paw —"

Suddenly the other children found their voices, and all started speaking at once.

"— and we've been feeding her —"

"— and she's going to have kittens —"

"— but we're not allowed to have pets —"

"— and the weather's getting too cold —"

"Whoa! Whoa!" shouted the mayor over the babble of voices. "One at a time!"

The children fell silent.

Now that he could make himself heard, the mayor looked right at Betsy and said, "This seems to be something of an emergency. Is that it?"

"Yes, sir," said Betsy. "She's going to have her kittens any day now. And if she has them outside, she'll hide them somewhere; and we won't be able to find them before winter comes."

"You know what I'd like to do?" the mayor asked.

"N—no, sir." Betsy's voice was small and scared.

"I'd *like* to insist that you children take those kittens in and give them decent homes."

Betsy gave a sigh of relief.

"*But*," continued the mayor, "there's only one catch."

Betsy and her friends exchanged worried looks.

"What's that?" asked Betsy.

"I don't make the rules. The City Council has to approve any change in the rules for the Project. You know, you're not the first ones who have said the rule against pets was unfair. Now I wonder what we could do about it." He was silent for a moment.

The children watched his face anxiously.

"Hm—m—m — yes. It just might work," he said at last. He looked at Betsy. "What's your name, little girl?"

"Who? Me?" Betsy looked around, hoping he meant some other child.

"Yes — you."

"Oh. Betsy."

"All right, Betsy. Do you think you could go in there to the City Council meeting and show them the petition just the way you showed it to me?"

"Oh — no!" Betsy stepped back toward the protection of the rest of the group. "I'd be too scared."

A Very Determined Young Lady

"You weren't too scared of me, were you, Betsy?" asked the mayor.

"No—o—o." She remembered that she *had* been afraid of him. But that seemed a little silly now. He was not a bit fierce.

"Do you want to keep that cat, Betsy?" he asked.

"Oh — yes! I do!"

Betsy bit her lip. That cat was certainly leading her into doing a lot of things she would have been too scared to do last year — writing a petition, ringing all those strange doorbells to get signatures, talking to the mayor. And now he wanted her to face the City Council! Well, she'd come this far. She couldn't give up now.

"All right. I *guess* I could do it," she said.

"That's the girl!" exclaimed the mayor.

As Betsy and the mayor entered the room, the council members went back to their seats. Betsy almost changed her mind when she saw all those strange grown-up faces staring at her from around the big council-room table. The council members looked like the kind of people who could say "No" to almost anything.

The mayor sat down in the chair at the head of the table and told her to stand beside him. He rapped on the table for silence.

"I'd like to make a change in the order of business," he said. "I want to introduce a very determined young lady to you. Her name is Betsy — uh — Betsy, what's your last name?"

"Delaney."

"Her name is Betsy Delaney, and she has a problem for you."

To be called "determined" made Betsy feel a

little braver. She tried not to think of all those grown-up eyes looking at her. She tried to think instead of the cat's green eyes.

Once she started talking, it was not as hard as she had thought it would be to explain about the petition and the lame cat the children had been feeding. When she had finished and had passed the petition for all of them to examine, the mayor motioned to her to lean closer to him.

He whispered in her ear, "This isn't a promise, Betsy, but if I were you, I'd go home and catch that cat and lock her up before she starts having kittens all over the place."

Betsy grinned. "Oh, yes, sir!" she said.

As she turned to leave, she saw the mayor very distinctly wink at her. She winked back. It seemed silly now that she had been so scared of him at first.

The newspaper lay on the hall floor just outside the door to Betsy's apartment when she came home from school the next day. Betsy snatched it up. She searched through it until she found a short paragraph at the bottom of the fifth page.

"City Council changes rule to allow pets in housing project," it started.

AUTHOR

"A Visit to the Mayor" is from Nellie Burchardt's popular book, *Project Cat.* Mrs. Burchardt lives on Staten Island, New York, and enjoys writing about city children. She once worked as a librarian in New York City but is now a housewife and the mother of two daughters.

Mrs. Burchardt likes to think of stories while she is doing her housework. She says, "It blocks out my 'I don't want to do dishes' thoughts." When she sits down for lunch, she writes out her ideas so she won't forget them. Mrs. Burchardt then tries out her stories on her own children. She feels that they are good judges of what other young people will like to read and says they often make useful suggestions.

Besides *Project Cat,* you will also enjoy reading *Reggie's No-Good Bird,* another book about a city housing project.

MAGIC WORDS TO FEEL BETTER

a song of the Netsilik Eskimos

SEA GULL
who flaps his wings
over my head
          in the blue air,
you GULL up there
dive down
          come here
take me with you
          in the air!

Wings flash by
my mind's eye
and I'm up there sailing
in the cool air,
          a-a-a-a-a-ah,
               in the air.

— Nakasuk

39

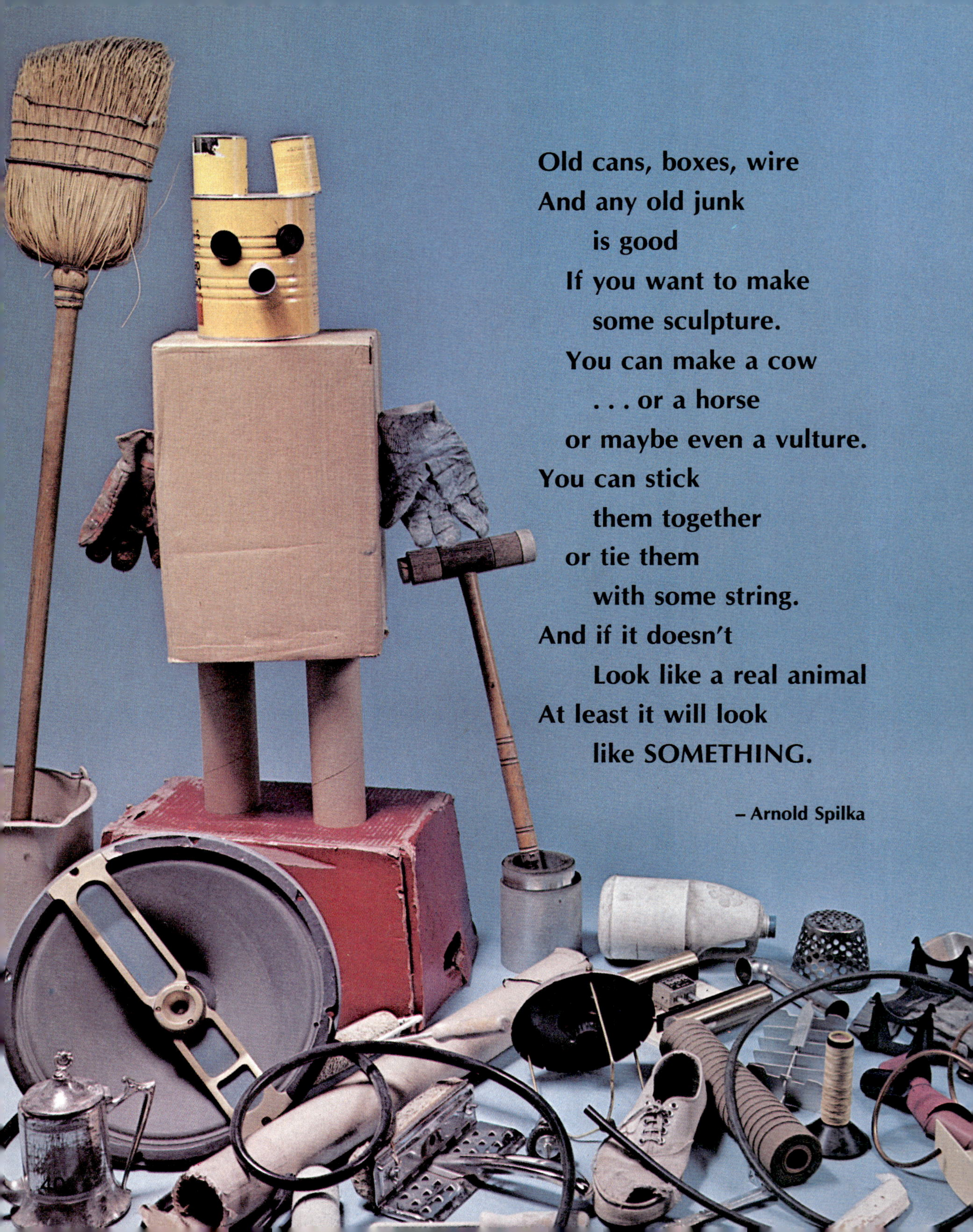

Old cans, boxes, wire
And any old junk
      is good
   If you want to make
      some sculpture.
   You can make a cow
      . . . or a horse
      or maybe even a vulture.
   You can stick
      them together
   or tie them
      with some string.
   And if it doesn't
      Look like a real animal
   At least it will look
      like SOMETHING.

– Arnold Spilka

**Skill
Lesson:**

RECOGNIZING AND
UNDERSTANDING SIMILES

Suppose you wanted to tell someone what a fast runner a friend of yours is. Here are two sentences that you might use:

1. Joe can run faster than anyone else I know.

2. Joe can run as fast as a deer.

Each of those sentences says that Joe is a fast runner. Sentence 1 compares Joe with other people. It says that Joe can run faster than other people. Sentence 2 also compares Joe with something else, but it compares him with a deer instead of comparing him with people.

When we compare things that are *alike* in most ways, we are making a **simple comparison.** In Sentence 1, Joe, who is a person, is compared with other persons.

Since all persons are alike in most ways, the comparison between Joe and other persons is a simple comparison.

In Sentence 2, however, the comparison is between a person and a deer. Here the comparison is between things that are not alike. A comparison between quite *different* things is called a **simile** (sim′uh-lee).

Here are more examples of similes:

3. Mother was as busy as a bee.
4. That boy is slower than a turtle.
5. Bill ate his lunch like a starved bear.
6. Sarah jumped over the fence like a grasshopper.

Notice that in Sentence 3 the word *as* is used in making the comparison. In Sentence 4, the word *than* is used. In Sentences 5 and 6, the word *like* is used. When you see two things compared by using the words *as, than,* or *like* in your reading, remember that you may be reading a simile.

Very often a writer uses a simile to make such things as the speed or size of something stand out very clearly. That's because, in a simile, the *one* way in which the two things are alike stands out in your mind. In a simple comparison, you might think of other ways in which the two things are alike. A simile makes a stronger comparison. Most people feel that similes are more interesting to read than simple comparisons. Certainly, a simile is more interesting than a simple statement like "Joe can run very fast."

Usually you will understand the meaning of a simile right away. If you don't, you can almost always figure out what the author is trying to tell you if you do these things:

A. Make sure you know what two things are being compared.
B. Think how those two things could be alike.
C. Choose the one way in which they are alike that will make the most sense in what you are reading.

See if you can do those three things now with the simile in each of the following sentences:

7. Jim's as lazy as an old dog lying in the sun.
8. Mary was as excited over her new chemistry set as a dog would be over a new bone.
9. Jane can sing like a bird.
10. When Bill looked out the airplane window, the cars and trucks below looked like toys.

Discussion

Help your class answer these questions:

1. What is the difference between a simple comparison and a simile?

2. Why do you think Joe was compared with a deer instead of a donkey?

3. What three words often show that a simile is being used?

4. Why do story writers often use similes?

5. What three things can you do to help you figure out the meaning of a simile?

6. In each of Sentences 3 through 10, what two things are being compared? How are those two things alike? What is the one likeness that the writer of each sentence was trying to tell you about?

On your own

Find the simile in each paragraph that follows. Then figure out what the speaker was trying to tell you by using that simile.

"John, your room is like a jungle," said Mr. Smith to his son. "I could hardly walk through to close the window this morning. After school today, I want you to pick up your things and put them away."

The conductor was leading the singing group in practice. Usually the singers did a good job, but today they were not doing well at all. They were singing much too loudly, and they were also out of tune. Finally the conductor exclaimed, "What's the matter with you people today? You sound like a bunch of braying donkeys!"

One evening, Ann's mother and father let her stay up late to watch a special show on TV. The next morning, she just couldn't seem to get going. Even after she washed up, she still felt sleepy. She was late getting to the breakfast table, and she took twice as long as usual to eat her eggs. Her mother finally said, "Ann, if you don't stop moving like a snail, you'll never get to school on time. Whatever is the matter with you?"

Checking your work

Talk with your class about the similes in the three paragraphs above. Decide whether or not you think each simile was a good way for the speaker in that paragraph to get his or her idea across.

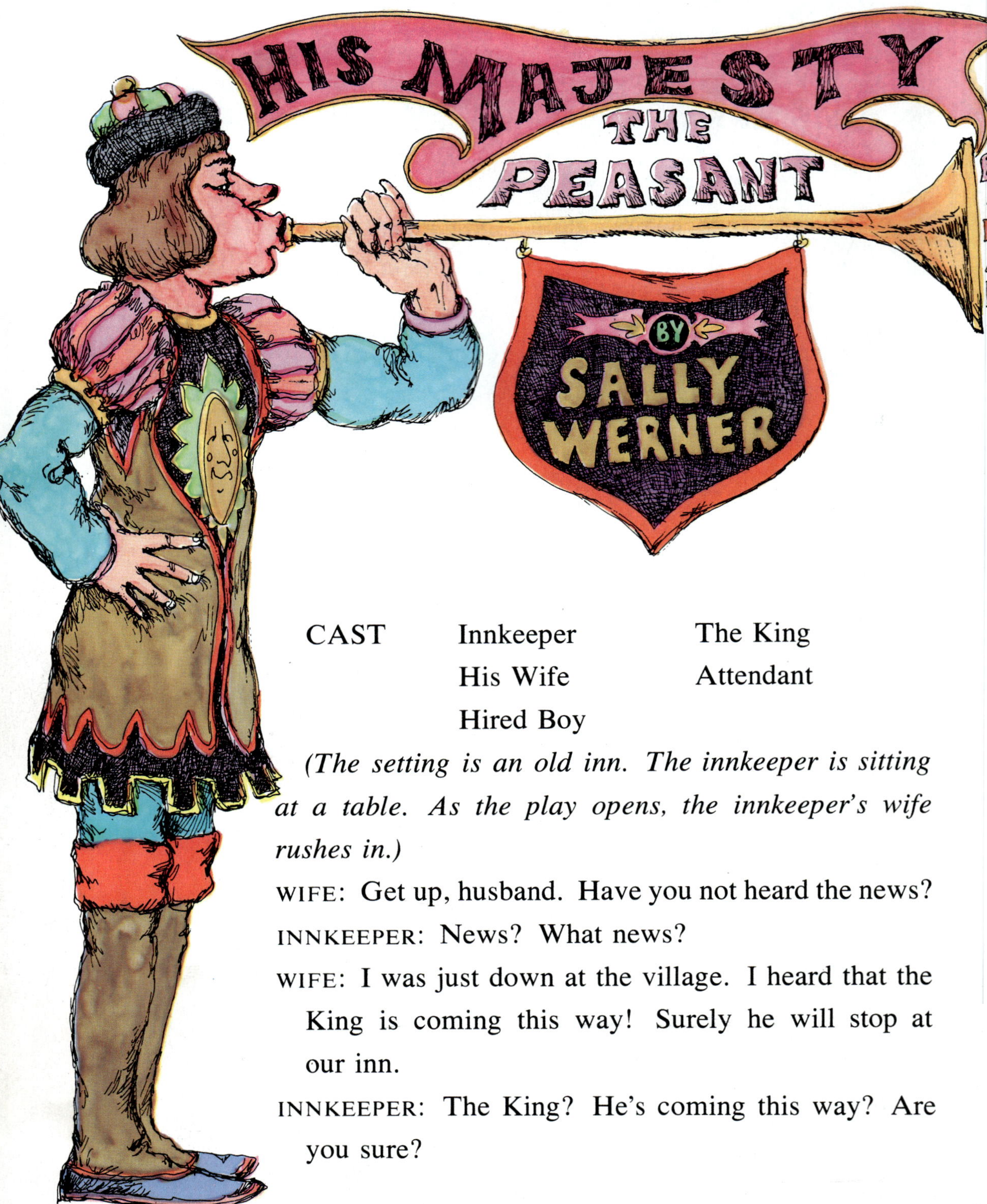

CAST	Innkeeper	The King
	His Wife	Attendant
	Hired Boy	

(The setting is an old inn. The innkeeper is sitting at a table. As the play opens, the innkeeper's wife rushes in.)

WIFE: Get up, husband. Have you not heard the news?

INNKEEPER: News? What news?

WIFE: I was just down at the village. I heard that the King is coming this way! Surely he will stop at our inn.

INNKEEPER: The King? He's coming this way? Are you sure?

WIFE: Indeed I am. He's coming soon. (*She grabs the broom.*) Hurry, we must clean. Where is that stupid servant boy?

INNKEEPER: He just stepped out to fetch a pail of water and some wood. Here he comes now. (*Hired boy enters with wood and water.*)

WIFE: (*To boy*) Here, Stupid! Don't just stand there. The King is coming! You must scrub the floor.

HIRED BOY: (*Putting down the wood and pail*) The King is coming? Here?

WIFE: Don't stand there and ask questions. Get to work! (*Hired boy begins to sweep.*)

INNKEEPER: We must have good bread for the King.
I'll go to the baker's down the road.

WIFE: And we must have fresh eggs. I'll gather them.
(*She turns to hired boy.*) Listen, boy. I'm putting
you in charge of cleaning the inn. If any people
stop here, tell them the King is coming and have
them help you clean. Do you hear?

HIRED BOY: I hear. Anyone who comes must help.
The King is coming.

WIFE: See that you have the inn spotless when we
return, or you will lose your job. And a job is
hard to come by these days. (*Hired boy gets to
work quickly as innkeeper and wife leave.*)

HIRED BOY: I must go get the scrub pail and brushes.
(*He leaves. King and Attendant enter.*)

ATTENDANT: Ah, what a cheerful inn, Your Majesty.
Do sit down, Sire. We have had a long journey.
I'm sure you are tired.

KING: Yes, it has been a long journey, but a good one.
It has been nice to get away from all the fuss and
ceremony. Not many people recognize me in these
clothes. The peasants look so happy! I wish I
could be a peasant, if only for a little while.

ATTENDANT: You are tired, Sire. Rest here while I
tend to the horses. You'll feel better after you rest.

49

(*Hired boy enters as attendant leaves.*)

HIRED BOY: Ah, I'm glad to see that someone has come. The innkeeper's wife said everyone must help to get ready for the King. He is coming this way very soon. So, my friend, please get ready to help me clean. The inn must be swept and scrubbed before the King comes.

KING: But — but — you don't know —

HIRED BOY: I don't know much, it's true. But there is no time for talk. Here, take this brush. I'll take the other one. We must scrub the floor beneath that table. The King will sit there.

KING: But, my good man —

HIRED BOY: I am not your good man! I am the hired boy. Come, get to work, or I will lose my job! Hurry, there's not much time. We must work together.

KING: (*Smiling*) It is for the King, eh? Well, give me the brush. Just how do I go about this?

HIRED BOY: You are more stupid than I am! Here, get down like this. (*They kneel under table.*) Hold the brush like this. Scrub back and forth until the floor is clean. (*King begins to scrub.*) Harder! You must press hard. Ah, you learn fast. You're doing fine. I'm sure if the innkeeper's wife saw you, she would hire you on the spot. I'll put in a good word for you.

KING: Thank you! Your compliment does me good. (*Hired boy whistles.*) Must I whistle, too?

HIRED BOY: Oh, it's much easier to work when you whistle. (*King whistles while he works. They look at each other and smile as they work. Innkeeper and wife enter.*)

INNKEEPER: The baker has nice fresh bread.

WIFE: And I gathered plenty of eggs. We shall fix a fine meal for the King. Ah, I see the boy has help.

(*Goes to King*) Scrub well under the table, and hurry. The King will be here soon. (*Attendant enters.*)

ATTENDANT: Ah, good day. We stopped for a bite to eat and to rest on our way to the castle. (*Looks around*) But where is His Majesty, the King?

INNKEEPER: The King?

HIRED BOY: (*Looks up from under table*) No king here. Just me and this good man who is helping

me. (*Attendant gasps as he looks under table at King. The King looks up smiling and then gets up.*)

ATTENDANT: (*Bowing*) Your Majesty!

WIFE: What? The King!

INNKEEPER: Not the King!

HIRED BOY: Are you — are you the King?

KING: Ah, that I am. But for a short time you have made me a peasant. And a good one, you said!

WIFE: Oh, what have you done, you stupid boy?

INNKEEPER: Yes, what have you done to the King? We are very sorry, Your Majesty. That stupid boy knows nothing.

KING: You call him stupid?

WIFE: Indeed we do.

KING: (*Speaks to hired boy*) Stupid One, you have made me do a peasant's work, and I enjoyed it. Moreover, I can see that you do your own work very well. I would like you to come to my palace and be in charge of the cleaning. We shall call you **KNIGHT STUPENDOUS!**

HIRED BOY: Oh, thank you, Sire!

KING: And now, Knight Stupendous, will you order food for us? You shall sit at my right while we eat. (*King, Attendant, and hired boy sit at table.*)

HIRED BOY: (*To the woman*) Come, good woman. Bring us food and drink. We must eat and be on our way.

WIFE: Yes, sir! (*To husband*) Come, help me get food and drink. Don't stand there staring. Come! (*They rush out to get food.*)

ATTENDANT: (*Comes to front of stage and bows to audience*) That is the end of the play, my friends. (*Turns toward King and hired boy and raises his hand*) Long live His Majesty, the Peasant!

AUTHOR

Sally Werner was born in Finland, and she came to the United States when she was seven years old. Mrs. Werner first began writing when she worked with the Girl Scouts and wrote plays for their puppet shows. She then decided to try writing for children's magazines, and she is still doing this successfully.

Mrs. Werner also worked as a nurse. After her husband died, she moved to Florida. Besides writing for magazines, Mrs. Werner keeps busy as chairman of a neighborhood group that puts on plays.

Easy Diver
Robert Froman

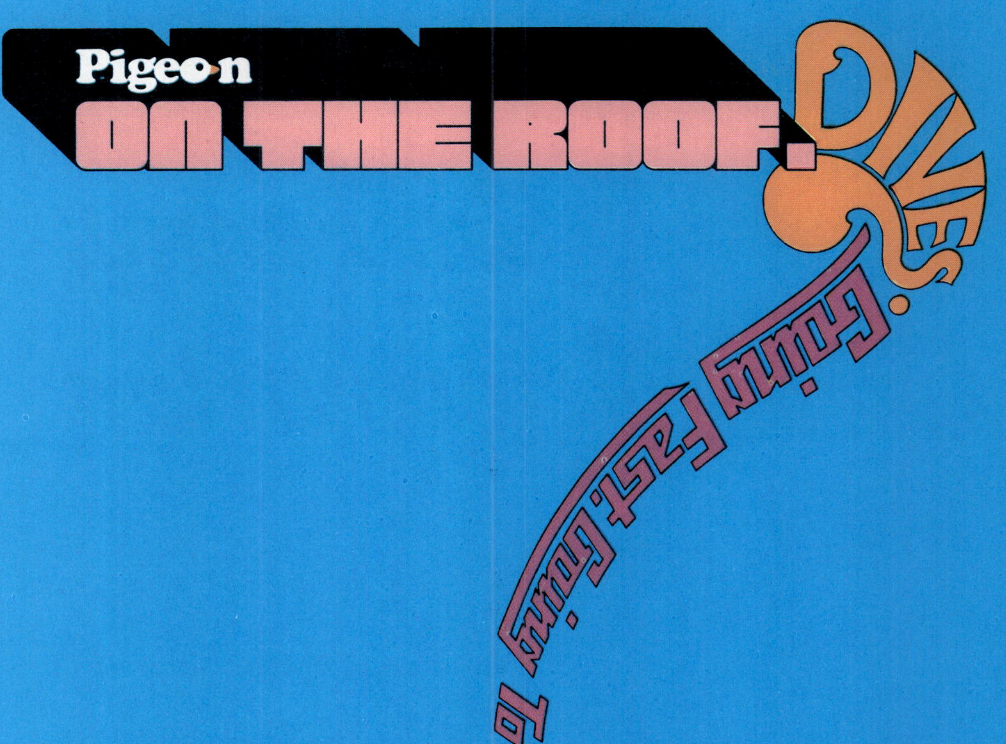

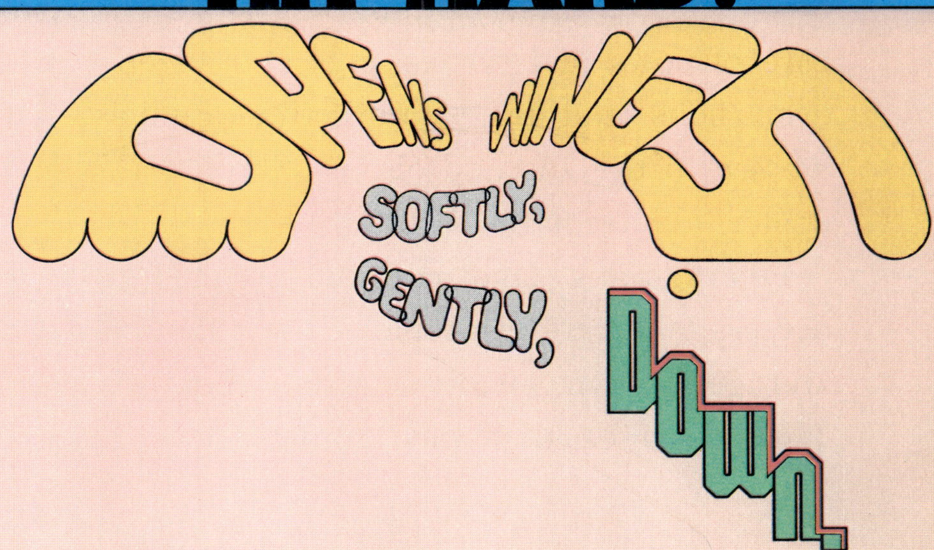

Dr. Penny, Veterinarian

by Gloria and Esther Goldreich

This is Dr. Penny. She is a special kind of doctor. Her patients are mostly cats and dogs, birds and bunnies. But she knows how to take care of cows and horses, pigs and sheep — and even lions and tigers and other animals that we see in the zoo and circus. She is an animal doctor, a veterinarian.

Veterinarians take care of animals just as doctors take care of people. They examine them and give them medicine when they are sick. They also see that the animals have general check-ups so that they stay healthy. They measure and weigh them, make sure they eat and drink the right things, and operate on them when they must.

Penny always wanted to take care of animals. When she was a little girl, she brought home stray cats and dogs and took care of them. She read many books about animals. Later, when she was older, she went to college and studied science. Then she went to a school of veterinary medicine. On graduation day she became Dr. Penny. She had to study hard but it was fun to learn, especially since she was studying something she loved.

Every morning Dr. Penny drives to work at an animal hospital. She arrives bright and early because she is anxious to see all the sick pets and make sure they are getting better. She and another doctor check the sick animals. When people get sick or need an operation, they go to a hospital. They usually sleep there and stay until they are better. Sick animals must do the same thing. Each animal in the hospital has its own clean, comfortable cage.

Princess, a cat, is ready to go home now that her ear infection is cured. A puppy is waiting

for its hurt paw to heal. A bunny named Peter is
hopping around again now that Dr. Penny has
made his stomach ache go away with some medicine. Another patient, a mother cat, had a hurt
tail, but now she is better and ready to go home
to her kittens.

After the doctors have checked all the patients,
they examine the new animals and decide how
to help them.

Rex's owner brought him to see Dr. Penny
because he was limping. She must find out

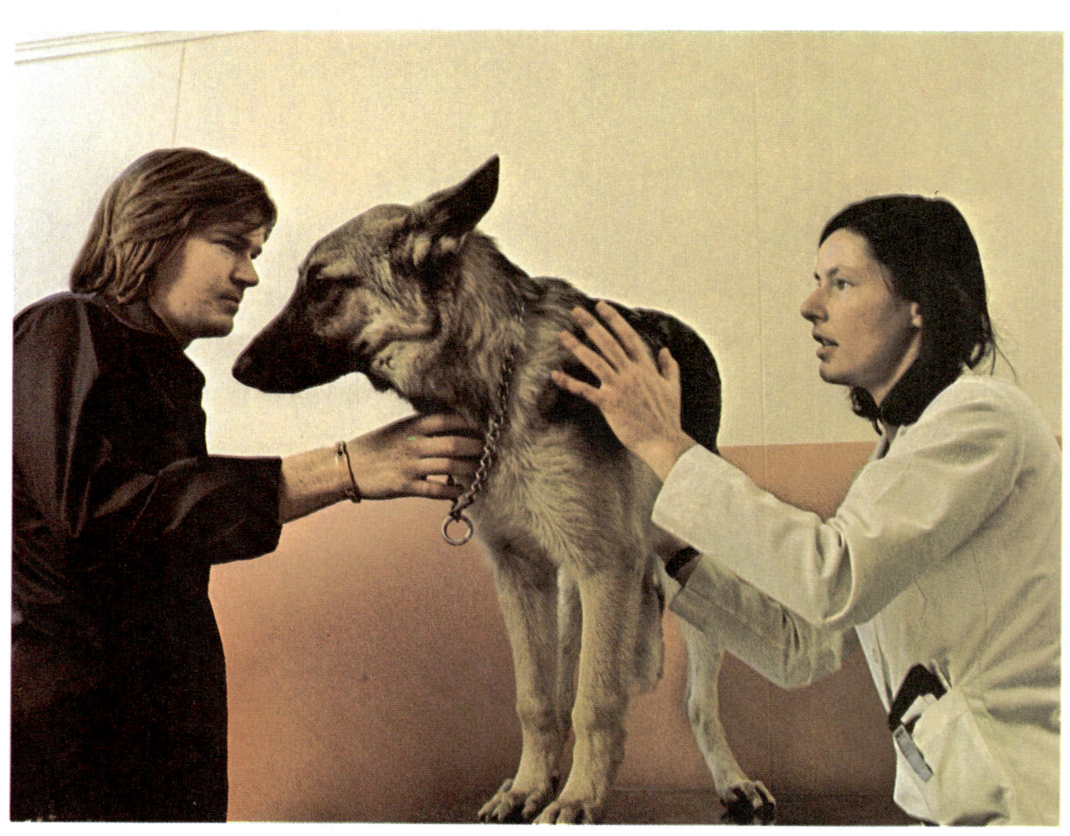

why Rex is dragging his right paw. Dr. Penny will examine him to determine the reason for the limp. Is his leg bruised? Is his paw infected? Perhaps he has hurt his bone.

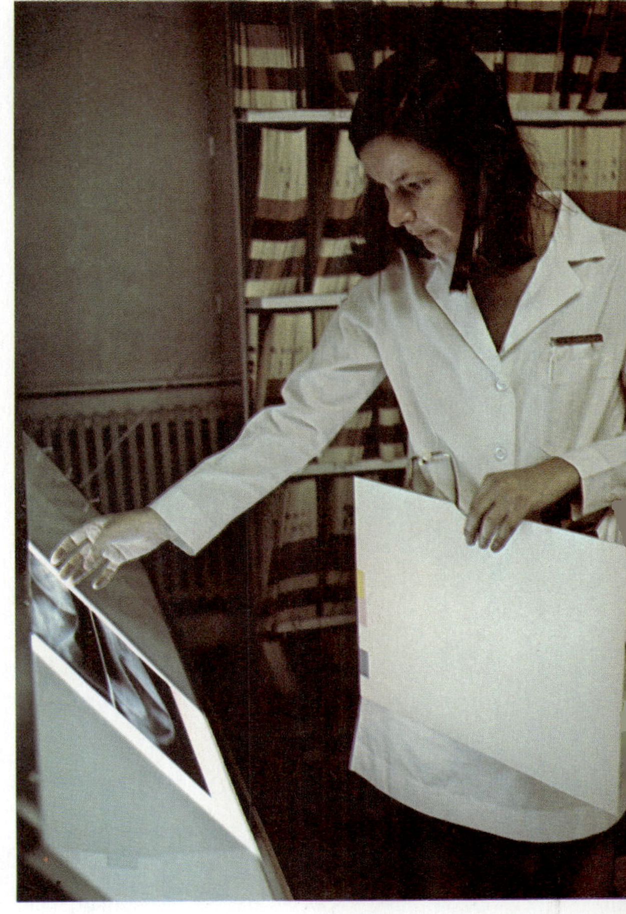

Dr. Penny decides to take a picture of the inside of Rex's leg with an X-ray machine. The rays of this machine are very strong so Dr. Penny wears a special apron to protect herself from them. When the X-ray picture is developed, she knows just what is wrong with Rex. His leg is fractured. Rex must have fallen or bumped into something and broken his bone. Dr. Penny will be able to mend the break with an operation.

Dr. Penny gets ready for the operation by washing her hands very carefully with hot water and a strong soap. This is to make sure

that no germs get on the dog. For the same
reason she wears a clean mask and cap, a sterile
gown, and rubber gloves. The operation does not
hurt Rex because Dr. Penny puts him to sleep
with an anesthetic — in this case a gas. While
he is asleep, she gives him oxygen to help him
breathe.

During the operation she inserts a pin to hold
the broken bone together. If Rex moves his leg
too much he may jerk the pin out of place, so
Dr. Penny puts a cast on to hold his leg straight
until it mends. Rex feels a bit uncomfortable

just now, but soon he will be ready to go home and frolic about on his lawn.

Dr. Penny spends a part of each morning in the laboratory. Sometimes she looks through a microscope to study slides. Today she puts a sample of a puppy's blood on a slide. The microscope has a glass that makes the blood cells look large enough for her to see them. Then Dr. Penny can tell what is wrong. This slide tells her that an infection is causing the puppy's fever. She gives him medicine to make him better.

Afternoons are very busy for Dr. Penny, because that is when most people bring their animals in to see her. Some children bring their pets in themselves. Sometimes a whole family brings a dog to see the veterinarian. The owners always seem more worried than the pets.

Dr. Penny gives some animals shots to prevent diseases that animals sometimes get. These injections are like the ones doctors give children so they will not get the mumps or measles. Animals get them for diseases like rabies or distemper. They don't always like their injections, but Dr. Penny and their owners know the injections are good for them.

Animal doctors are also animal dentists. It is part of their job to keep the animal's teeth clean. Certain animals are better patients than some children who go to the dentist.

Cats and dogs must have their eyes and ears checked, too. A look into their mouths tells Dr. Penny whether or not they have healthy gums and good strong teeth.

Snow White has hurt her shoulder. Dr. Penny puts a collar on her to keep her head straight so she cannot bite or move the bandage.

After Dr. Penny has examined the animals, she talks to their owners. She explains what has been bothering their pets and tells them how to take care of them. All the animal owners know it is very important to do exactly what the veterinarian says.

Sometimes there is a lot of excitement in an

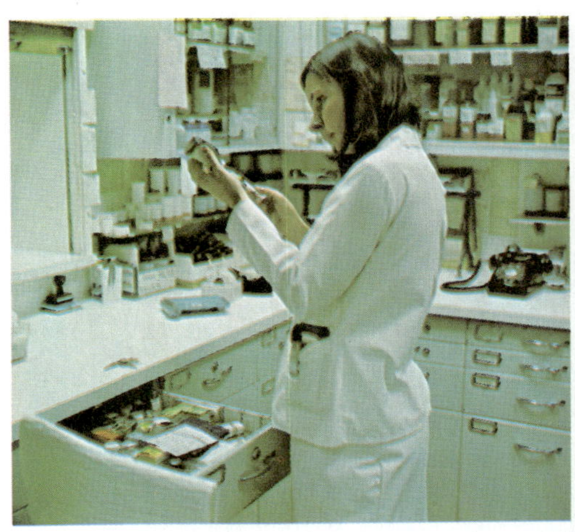

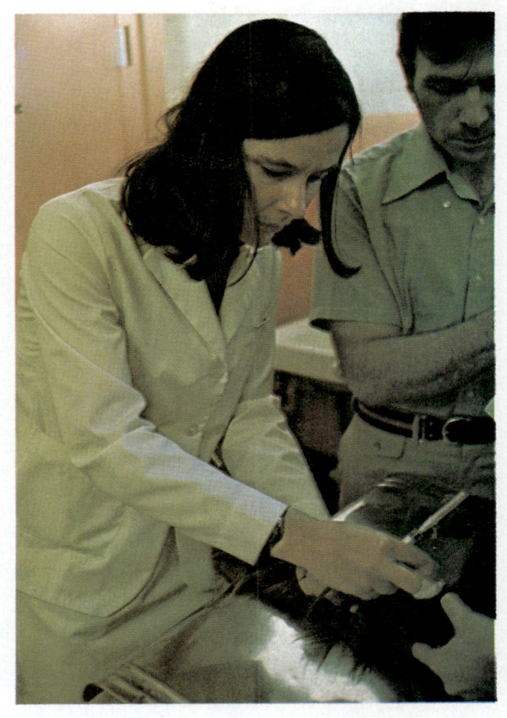

animal hospital. A dog named Sebastian was just hit by a car. His family rushed him to Dr. Penny's hospital. Peter and Katie have owned him since he was a little pup, and they are quite concerned about what will happen to him. Their grandmother is worried, too. She holds the leash nervously while Dr. Penny examines the frightened dog.

All is well. Sebastian is fine but a bit frightened. He has learned a good lesson. Next time he will not chase passing cars.

"You must not let your dog run out in the street," Dr. Penny tells the children. They promise they will be more careful, and Sebastian goes home with his happy family.

All afternoon Dr. Penny's phone rings. Owners call to ask about pets that are staying in the hospital. Children call to ask questions about what to feed their pets. Laboratories call with results of tests. The skin, bone, or blood samples Dr. Penny has sent them often tell her what is wrong with one of the animals.

At the end of the day Dr. Penny is tired. She has worked very hard and helped lots of animals. But when she gets home she is still ready to romp with her own dogs.

Dr. Penny loves her work. She is always busy helping her animals. Every day she learns something new about them. She thinks being a veterinarian is exciting and the very best kind of work for her to do.

AUTHORS

Gloria and Esther Goldreich are sisters and are both working women themselves. The article "Dr. Penny, Veterinarian" is from their book *What Can She Be? A Veterinarian*. They have also written *What Can She Be? A Lawyer* and *What Can She Be? A Newscaster*.

Esther Goldreich is a systems analyst who works with computers for Perathon Inc. She has many interests, such as digging in ancient ruins, dancing, tennis, and sailing.

Gloria Goldreich is a writer whose stories and articles have appeared in many magazines. She got the idea of writing the veterinarian book from her son and two daughters. "My children are quite interested in what people do all day," she says. "I wanted to give them some insight into a woman's work world."

Mystery Guest at Left End

by Beman Lord

The Packers had just lost their sixth football game in a row. They'd have had at least a tie if only Louie Williams, who played left end, could ever hold onto a ball once it was in his hands. As usual, he'd dropped the beautiful pass that Si had thrown him on the last play.

Walking home with his friend John Bradley, Si said, "What we need is a good left end, one who can catch a pass and hold onto it."

"I wish I could run faster," said John. "Maybe if I lost some of this weight . . ."

"Better not try!" Si said. "We need you, and especially that weight, on the line. We've just got to find another left end. Maybe one of us can come up with an idea in the next day or so. Be thinking about it!"

After lunch, Si decided to practice his throwing. He got his football and went out to the backyard. Two tires had been hung from trees. Si stood by one tire, took aim at the other, and threw the ball. It went nicely through the hoop. He then went over and picked up the ball, and

threw it back at the other tire. It sailed right through the hoop again.

"My aim is good," he said aloud. "All I need is someone to catch it."

"That shouldn't be too hard to do with those weak throws," said a voice.

Si looked around, trying to see who had spoken. He couldn't see anyone.

"It's harder than you think, whoever you are, and my throws are not weak."

There was no answer. He picked up the football, looked around again, even up at the trees, and threw the ball at the tire. It missed.

"Not only are the throws weak, but that one was crooked," the voice said calmly.

Si turned quickly, but he still couldn't see anybody. "I don't know who or where you are, but I'm getting sick and tired of your remarks. Either come out and show your face or keep your thoughts to yourself!"

"I'm only trying to be helpful," the voice answered. "And as far as I can see, you need more than a little help."

"It's hard to throw at an old tire," Si shouted back. Then he decided to change his tactics. "You're right. I do need help. How about catching a few passes?"

"Oh, all right. Now that you've asked nicely."

Si saw a girl get up from a lawn chair in the next yard. "I thought it sounded like a girl! But what's the idea of hiding behind a lawn chair?"

The girl crossed over to Si's yard. "My name is Faith Cummings, in case you've forgotten. Your mother introduced us last week. And I wasn't hiding. I've been reading, and I must say your talking has been very annoying."

"So sorry," Si said. "Now if you'll just get back to your own yard, I'll get on with my passing."

"Are you afraid I might be too good?" asked Faith. "As far as I can see, there shouldn't be any problem catching a football. A girl should be able to do it as well as a boy. I've also watched football on TV with my father, so I do have some idea of the game."

"Okay! Okay, Miss Know-it-all, we'll give you a try," Si said, as he picked up the football. "Start running, and I'll throw the ball ahead of you."

Faith started running and was almost across her own backyard before Si threw. It was an excellent pass, and Faith caught it easily.

"Beginner's luck!" Si called. "Stay out there and I'll throw you another."

She caught a short one and a long one and a high one. Si was amazed, then more amazed, and finally flabbergasted.

"Good grief! Who'd have believed it!" he said, under his breath. He then threw her three more passes. She caught them all.

"Do you mind if I rest for a minute? All this running is making me hot." She didn't wait for an answer, but quickly sat down.

Si walked over and pulled up another chair beside her. "I'd better apologize," he said. "Where did you ever learn to catch a football?"

"Nowhere. I can catch a softball quite well, and I didn't think a football would be too difficult.

I've always wanted to try. Thank you. Now, if you don't mind, I think I'll go back to my reading. Would you try to be a little quieter?"

"Will I try to be *what*? Are you crazy? Just because you can catch a football like nobody else, you want me to . . ." Si didn't finish the sentence. Suddenly his temper lessened. What an idea! Would it work? He'd have to talk it over with John. He started toward the house. Halfway there he turned and called politely, "You know, you were good."

"Yes, I know it. Thank you," she answered, without looking up from her book.

Si made a face and went into the house.

The Secret Deal

When John answered the telephone, Si said, "Drop whatever you're doing and get over here quickly. I think I've found a left end."

"Who?" John asked. "Where'd he come from? Has he just moved into town?"

"Came in last week. No more questions. Just get over here on the double. She might leave. I mean, it might leave. It's temperamental." Si was getting confused. "Just get over here." He hung up.

Si went out to the front porch. Within five minutes, John arrived.

"Where is he?" he asked, as he came up onto the porch. "I want to see him catch."

"Sit down, John," Si said very seriously. "I think I'd better tell you how it all started. Don't interrupt until I finish."

But when Si came to the part where Faith had come over to his yard, John burst out, "You mean to tell me that Faith Cummings is our new left end? You got me away from the Ohio State-Purdue game to tell me this? A girl! I lost five pounds just running over here."

"Hold your horses until I finish the story. It's

unbelievable," Si said. He quickly told John the rest. "I threw seven passes, and she didn't miss once. Imagine what we would do with her on the team!"

"I don't believe it. I've got to see it done. Let's go," John said, as he got up from his chair.

"Hold it," Si said. "I have a plan. She's pretty touchy. I'll flatter her into catching a few more, and then you come around the house quietly and watch. She might not do it if we both went back there together."

Faith was still reading. She looked up as Si came up to her chair, but she didn't say anything.

"I hate to interrupt you, but you were terrific! I still can't believe what I saw. Would you mind catching a few more passes?" Si asked politely.

Faith sighed. "Oh, all right," she said. "Do you think three or four would be enough? I would like to finish this book sometime today."

"Thanks. Stay right here and I'll get the ball." As he raced over to his yard, he noticed John

coming quietly up between the two houses. He gave him a nod and picked up the ball.

"Cut across your lawn slowly," Si yelled. "The ball will be waiting for you."

Faith did so and without any trouble caught the ball. Si threw her another. She caught it. The next two she also caught.

"I think that should prove to you that it wasn't beginner's luck," she said, as she walked back to her chair. "After all, I haven't missed one yet."

Si dashed around the house and motioned for John to follow him to the front porch. "Well," Si said, "do you believe it now? She hasn't missed once. Can you imagine how many games we could have won with her on our side?"

John shook his head. "I can't believe it. How does she do it?"

"The question isn't *how* does she do it — she *does* it, period. The question is will she do it for the team?" Si said. "I've been thinking. If we dressed her up in my brother's old uniform, no one would ever know she was a girl."

"It's touch football, so she won't be tackled," John said, warming up to the idea. "It certainly is worth a try. We've got to do something if the Packers are ever going to win a game. You ask her, and I'll back you up. Try flattering her again."

John and Si approached the lawn chair nervously. Si spoke first. "This is my friend, John Bradley. We're sorry to bother you, but could you give us five minutes of your time?"

She nodded to John. "Nice to meet you. Please sit down." She looked at her watch. "Three minutes is all I can spare. I still have the lunch dishes to do, and my mother will be fussing about them.''

The boys pulled up chairs, and Si explained the problem. He ended by saying, ''We need a good left end. You'd be sensational. We thought, and hoped, that you might help us out for our last two games.'' Si paused and waited for a reply. Faith just looked at both of them.

''You could wear Si's brother's uniform, and no one would know you're a girl,'' John said.

Faith glared at John. "I'm rather proud to be a girl."

"Well, look at it this way," Si said. "You could be our mystery guest."

She sat up. "How much do you pay?"

"Pay!" Si yelled. "This is for sport. We don't get paid anything. We do it for the fun."

"I agree you do it for the fun, but for me it's a different matter. I imagine there will be some work involved — practice and all that — and mystery guests do get paid."

John and Si looked at each other. "We don't have much money," John said weakly.

"It doesn't have to be money," Faith answered. "Just let me think for a minute."

While she was thinking, her mother came to the back door and called, "Faith, you haven't forgotten the dishes?"

"No, Mother. I'll be right there." Her mother closed the door, and Faith said to the boys, "If there's one thing I hate to do, it's dishes. Perhaps you'd like to help?"

"How much?" Si asked.

Faith smiled. "All right, I'll be your left end, and you two will be my dishwashers."

"What are you going to tell your folks?" John
asked.

"I'll tell them we have a secret deal," Faith
said.

"That's just the point," Si exclaimed. "If we
decide to do it, you'll have to promise to keep it
a secret."

Faith shrugged. "I promise. Now, if you'd like
to talk it over before you decide, today's dishes
can wait another minute."

The boys walked over to Si's yard, talked for a
few minutes, and returned. "I'll wash," said Si,
"and John will dry. Lead the way."

"George" Joins the Team

Friday night Si brought over the uniform.

"I'll try it on in the cellar," said Faith. A few minutes later she reappeared. "It fits fine."

"Good," Si said. "John and I will be by tomorrow about 8:30, and we'll all go down to the field together. Be ready then, okay?"

"It's rather early, but I'll be ready. After all, you've kept your share of the bargain, and I'll keep mine."

The next morning Faith appeared dressed in the football uniform and helmet, carrying a pocketbook and wearing pink slippers.

"Good grief! Are you nutty?" John cried, pointing to her shoes and pocketbook.

"I thought you might enjoy a little joke, but I can see you don't. You do take this game seriously." She disappeared and then came back wearing sneakers.

"Now let me do all the talking when we get there," Si said, as they started for the field. "Just remember you're my cousin visiting for the weekend and your name is George Matthews. You won't start the game, but you'll play when we need you. You're shy, and you don't like to talk. Just be sure you keep your promise about not telling you're a girl. And keep your ponytail under your helmet!"

When they reached the field, Si introduced the new player to the team. The game started with Faith, or George, on the bench. She didn't play the first quarter at all, but she played off and on the rest of the game. She caught five out of five passes, made two touchdowns, and gained many, many yards. The Packers won their first game. The team crowded around Faith and kept patting her on the back. Si and John tried to get her away before anyone could realize she was a girl. They were also not sure

how much pounding she could take before
losing her temper. They finally got her away and
started for home.

"This calls for a celebration," Si said, as they
left the field. "We'll all stop at Pete's Drugstore,
and I'll do the treating. You were just great,
George!"

"Thank you, but you now can call me Faith.
I was rather good, don't you think, John?"

"You were a pro," John said. "You fooled
everybody. Those Steelers never knew *what* a
mystery guest we had!"

They reached the drugstore and found a table in the back. Faith started to remove her helmet.

"Do you want to give the whole thing away?" Si exclaimed. "I know it'll be uncomfortable eating ice cream, but could you leave it on for another ten minutes?"

Faith said, "All right. I'll have a hot fudge sundae with strawberry ice cream."

"That's forty cents!" Si said. "I wasn't planning to celebrate quite *that* much. But it isn't every day that the Packers win a game." They gave their order, and after a few minutes the waitress brought it.

"I just love these sundaes and never seem to get enough of them. I could eat one every day of the week," said Faith.

"Boy, wait until next week and we win another one," John said to Si. "We should have had her playing for us the whole season."

Faith put down her spoon. "I didn't want to talk business while we were eating. But now that you've brought up the matter of next week's game, there's one small question. How much?"

"The usual fee," Si said. "Dishes for a week."

"My mother says you are not getting them clean enough. However, I do happen to have

another idea. These sundaes are delicious.
Starting tomorrow, I'd like a standing order of
one every day next week."

"Why, that's . . ." John said, counting on his
fingers. "That's $2.80!"

"Very good," Faith answered. "$1.40 apiece.
You said yourself I was a pro."

John and Si looked at each other. "Okay," Si
said halfheartedly. "You can have a sundae
every day."

"Thank you," said Faith. "And now I must
run. I'll see you on Tuesday and Thursday for
practice."

Both boys nodded.

Decoy

As Si and John were walking to Faith's house on Tuesday, Si said, "I've been worrying about Faith and next Saturday's game. Do you realize they'll be out to get her on every play?"

John stopped dead in his tracks. "We need her to catch your passes! But on the other hand, we wouldn't want her to get hurt."

After talking some more, they decided to tell Faith that she shouldn't play. While they waited for her to come out of her house, Si said, "Don't feel too bad, John. We did win one game this season."

When Faith appeared, Si said, "John and I have been talking about Saturday's game. It's going to be rougher, and they'll try to block you on every play, after last week's game. We both think it might be better if you didn't play, and we're releasing you from our bargain."

Faith started to laugh and then realized how serious the boys were. "I'm sorry, but you know I'm not all that tender. And I took quite a few blocks in the last game. Thanks for the offer, but I'm going to play."

"Do you realize you're going to be a sitting duck?" John exclaimed.

"Yes," Faith said, "a sitting duck and probably a decoy, too."

"You both have said the magic words!" cried Si. "I think everything's going to be all right. We are going to have a mystery guest decoy."

George, or Faith, turned out to be exactly that in the game. Si used her for only two plays in the first quarter. The Steelers naturally expected a pass and guarded her. Si faked passing both times and ran with the ball. The first play netted twenty yards, and the second play brought the Packers a touchdown. He didn't use her in the second or third quarters, but then in the last quarter the Steelers tied it up. Si called George in and called time out.

"We're confusing them," Si said to the team. "George will go out for a pass. Most of their backfield will be guarding him and the rest rushing me. I'll throw to Ernie and he'll run around the right end. Let's go!"

The play worked exactly as Si said it would, and they gained fifteen yards.

"Good, we're getting there." Si patted Ernie on the back. "We're really confusing them. This time, I'll throw to George."

The team broke from the huddle and took their

places on the line. George, or Faith, was playing
a wide left end. She had figured that this gave
her freedom to get around her blocker and
either run left or right of him. She heard the
signal, sidestepped her blocker, and raced down
the field. She ran straight for about ten yards
and then cut across the field.

Si spotted her and threw the ball. When she
saw that it was going over her head, she ran back
and made a jump for the ball. She couldn't get
hold of it, and it bounced off her fingers into
the hands of Bob Taylor, the Packers' right end.
Bob had tried to pull the Steelers away from

"George" by pretending the pass was coming to him, but it hadn't worked. He had then raced across the field to give "George" blocking. He never broke his stride as the ball landed in his hands, and he raced for a touchdown.

As she came down from her jump, Faith was off balance, and she stumbled into the Steelers' halfback. The force threw her to the ground, and her helmet came tumbling off. She sprang to her feet.

"Of all the nerve! Why don't you watch where you're going?" she said to the amazed Steeler.

"I was standing still!" Then he realized what he was seeing. "Fellows," he yelled. "George is a girl! He's that new girl!"

Both teams gathered around. John and Si stood back, waiting to hear the razzing. It didn't come. Instead they heard:

"A girl? Who would have thought it?"

"Where did you learn to catch like that?"

"Will you play for us next year?"

Faith listened for a while and then said, "Thank you for all the compliments. But I believe I've had enough football for this or any year. Now, if you'll excuse me, you can get back to your game." She picked up her helmet, smiled at John and Si, and walked off the field.

All the boys watched her go and gave her a round of applause. She turned and waved.

No one scored in the last minutes of the game. The Packers won 13–6.

After the game, John said to Si, "The celebration is on me today." As they walked into Pete's, there sat Faith, all alone, eating her last hot fudge sundae.

She signaled to them, and the boys went over and joined her. "I'm almost finished, but I wanted to say thank you for the sundaes."

"We want to thank you for keeping your part of the bargain. You played a terrific game," John said.

She finished the last of her ice cream and stood up. "Thank you. I did, didn't I? Girls can be useful sometimes, don't you think? Now I'm going to get out of this uniform and into some decent clothes."

The boys didn't say anything. John ordered and they just sat there. The waitress brought their order and left. Each picked up a straw and started to drink from the one bottle of soda pop.

Finally Si said, "You don't suppose she plays basketball, do you?"

AUTHOR

Beman Lord wrote *Mystery Guest at Left End* for his nieces, who complained that there weren't enough girls in his stories! There is also a girl in *Shot Put Challenge*. But all of Beman Lord's sports books are popular with both boys and girls. Two of them — *Quarterback's Aim* and *The Trouble with Francis* — have won awards from the Boys Clubs of America. Some of his other books are *Bats and Balls, Guards for Matt*, and a science-fiction book called *The Day the Spaceship Landed*.

Beman Lord, his wife, and their two children live in New York City. Mr. Lord says of his own writing, "What I am trying to say in all my stories is that sports can be fun, and you don't have to be a great athlete to play them. I wasn't. I am thin and wear glasses. Yet I played all sports and had a good time."

Lewis Has a Trumpet

A trumpet

A trumpet

Lewis has a trumpet

A bright one that's yellow

A loud proud horn.

He blows it in the evening

When the moon is newly rising

He blows it when it's raining

In the cold and misty morn

It honks and it whistles

It roars like a lion

It rumbles like a lion

With a wheezing huffing hum

His parents say it's awful

Oh really simply awful

But

Lewis says he loves it

It's such a handsome trumpet

And when he's through with trumpets

He's going to buy a drum.

–Karla Kuskin

**Skill
Lesson:**

RECOGNIZING AND
UNDERSTANDING METAPHORS

Can you find the simile in the following sentence?

> On the school playground, Paul is usually as noisy as a howling dog.

You can see that Paul is being compared to a howling dog. The simile tells you that Paul is very noisy on the playground. The word *as* coming before and after *noisy* helps you to know that "as noisy as a howling dog" is a simile.

Now read the next sentence:

> 1. When Paul gets back to the classroom, however, he becomes a quiet little mouse.

That sentence says that Paul turns into a mouse when

he comes back to class. You know that such a thing could not really happen. Boys just don't turn into mice. The writer left out the signal words *as* or *like* and expected you to think them to yourself. The writer could have used the simile "... becomes *as* quiet *as* a little mouse." But perhaps the metaphor gets the idea across more strongly because it says something that just couldn't be true.

When a comparison of two different things is made without using the words *as, than,* or *like,* that comparison is called a **metaphor.**

When a writer says that something acts in a way you know is impossible, that may also be a metaphor. For example, think what the word *flew* in this sentence means:

> 2. Jack flew around the corner with the other boys after him.

Could a boy really fly unless he was in an airplane? No! The word *flew* in that sentence is telling you that Jack went around the corner so fast that his feet didn't seem to touch the ground at all. In that way Jack was like a flying bird. The word *flew* in that sentence is a metaphor.

A writer is also using a metaphor when describing someone or something with words that you know couldn't really be true of that person or thing. For

example, notice the word *gold* in the following description:

3. He had a heart of gold.

Are people's hearts ever made of gold? No! The writer wants you to know that the man was very kind-hearted, by comparing his kindness to the richness of gold.

When a word or group of words says something you know couldn't actually be true, remember that it may be a metaphor. You should make sure you know what the writer is trying to tell you in that metaphor. Usually you will know right away. If you don't, try doing these things:

A. Make sure you know what word or group of words says something that couldn't be true.
B. Think what two things the writer wants you to compare with each other.
C. Think how those two things might be alike.
D. Decide which of the ways in which they might be alike makes the most sense in what you are reading.

See if you can do those four things now with the
metaphors in each of the following sentences:

4. The house had so little furniture in it that it was
   just a big old barn.
5. From then until the bell rang, Bobby was a busy
   little beaver.
6. After supper, Father felt sorry he'd been so bad-
   tempered and said, "I hope you'll forgive me for
   having been such a bear this afternoon."
7. The moon was peeking shyly over the tops of the
   hills to the east.
8. Joe glued his eyes to the magician's hands, but he
   still couldn't figure out where all those colored
   handkerchiefs were coming from.
9. His velvet voice has made him a real success as a
   radio singer.

Discussion

Help your class answer these questions:
1. How is a metaphor like a simile? How is it different?
2. How can you tell when you may be reading a
   metaphor?
3. Why do writers often use metaphors?
4. What three things can you do to help you figure out
   the meaning of a metaphor?

5. In each of Sentences 4 through 9, what is the metaphor? What two things are being compared in each of those metaphors? How are those two things alike?

On your own

Find the metaphor in each of the following sentences, and figure out what the speaker or writer means by using that metaphor.

1. Mr. Lee's friend said, "Pete, your store has turned out to be a gold mine, hasn't it?"
2. "Stop repeating every single word I say, you parrot!" said Jim to his baby brother.
3. The ball jumped right out of the boy's glove.
4. The walls were so dirty that they cried out for someone to use some soap and water on them.
5. The barn door groaned loudly on its hinges as we pushed it open.
6. The look she gave him was so icy that he knew something he said must have hurt her feelings.

Checking your work

If you are asked to do so, tell what the metaphor is in one of the above sentences. Then help your class decide whether that metaphor was a good way for the writer to get his or her idea across.

Beware, My Child

Beware, my child,
of the snaggle-toothed beast.
He sleeps till noon,
then makes his feast
on Hershey bars
and cakes of yeast
and anyone around — o.

So when you see him,
sneeze three times
and say three loud
and senseless rhymes
and give him all your
saved-up dimes,
or else you'll ne'er be found — o.

— SHEL SILVERSTEIN

From

WINNIE-THE-POOH

by
A. A. MILNE

Pooh and Piglet Go Hunting
and Nearly Catch a Woozle

The Piglet lived in a very grand house in the middle of a beech-tree, and the beech-tree was in the middle of the forest, and the Piglet lived in the middle of the house. Next to his house was a piece of broken board which had: "TRES-PASSERS W" on it. When Christopher Robin asked the Piglet what it meant, he said it was his grandfather's name, and had been in the family for a long time. Christopher Robin said you *couldn't* be called Trespassers W, and Piglet said yes, you could, because his grandfather was, and it was short for Trespassers Will, which was short of Trespassers William. And his grandfather had had two names in case he lost one — Trespassers after an uncle, and William after Trespassers.

"I've got two names," said Christopher Robin carelessly.

"Well, there you are, that proves it," said Piglet.

One fine winter's day when Piglet was brushing away the snow in front of his house, he happened to look up, and there was Winnie-the-Pooh. Pooh was walking round and round in a circle, thinking of something else, and when Piglet called to him, he just went on walking.

"Hallo!" said Piglet. "What are *you* doing?"

"Hunting," said Pooh.

"Hunting what?"

"Tracking something," said Winnie-the-Pooh very mysteriously.

"Tracking what?" said Piglet, coming closer.

"That's just what I ask myself. I ask myself, What?"

"What do you think you'll answer?"

"I shall have to wait until I catch up with it," said Winnie-the-Pooh. "Now, look there." He pointed to the ground in front of him. "What do you see there?"

"Tracks," said Piglet. "Paw-marks." He gave a little squeak of excitement. "Oh, Pooh! Do you think it's a — a — a Woozle?"

"It may be," said Pooh. "Sometimes it is, and sometimes it isn't. You never can tell with paw-marks."

With these few words he went on tracking, and Piglet, after watching him for a minute or two, ran after him. Winnie-the-Pooh had come to a sudden stop, and was bending over the tracks in a puzzled sort of way.

"What's the matter?" asked Piglet.

"It's a very funny thing," said Bear, "but there seem to be *two* animals now. This — whatever-it-was — has been joined by another — whatever-it-is — and the two of them are now proceeding in company. Would you mind coming with me, Piglet, in case they turn out to be Hostile Animals?"

Piglet scratched his ear in a nice sort of way, and said that he had nothing to do until Friday, and would be delighted to come, in case it really *was* a Woozle.

"You mean, in case it really is two Woozles," said Winnie-the-Pooh, and Piglet said that anyhow he had nothing to do until Friday. So off they went together.

There was a small spinney of larch trees just here, and it seemed as if the two Woozles, if that is what they were, had been going round this spinney; so round this spinney went Pooh and Piglet after them; Piglet passing the time by telling Pooh what his Grandfather Trespassers W had done to Remove Stiffness after Tracking, and how his Grandfather Trespassers W had suffered in his later years from Shortness of Breath, and other matters of interest, and Pooh wondering what a Grandfather was like, and if perhaps this was Two Grandfathers they were after now, and, if so, whether he would be allowed to take one home and keep it, and what Christopher Robin would say. And still the tracks went on in front of them. . . .

Suddenly Winnie-the-Pooh stopped, and pointed excitedly in front him. *"Look!"*

"What?" said Piglet, with a jump. And then, to show that he hadn't been frightened, he jumped up and down once or twice in an exercising sort of way.

"The tracks!" said Pooh. *"A third animal has joined the other two!"*

"Pooh!" cried Piglet. "Do you think it is another Woozle?"

"No," said Pooh, "because it makes different marks. It is either Two Woozles and one, as it might be, Wizzle, or Two, as it might be, Wizzles and one, if so it is, Woozle. Let us continue to follow them."

So they went on, feeling just a little anxious now, in case the three animals in front of them were of Hostile Intent. And Piglet wished very much that his Grandfather T. W. were there, instead of elsewhere, and Pooh thought how nice it would be if they met Christopher Robin suddenly but quite accidentally, and only because he liked Christopher Robin so much. And then, all of a sudden, Winnie-the-Pooh stopped again, and licked the tip of his nose in a cooling manner, for he was feeling more hot and anxious than ever in his life before. *There were four animals in front of them!*

"Do you see, Piglet? Look at their tracks! Three, as it were, Woozles, and one, as it was, Wizzle. *Another Woozle has joined them!*"

And so it seemed to be. There were the tracks; crossing over each other here, getting muddled up with each other there; but, quite plainly every now and then, the tracks of four sets of paws.

"I *think*," said Piglet, when he had licked the tip of his nose too, and found that it brought very little comfort, "I *think* that I have just remembered something. I have just remembered something that I forgot to do yesterday and shan't be able to do tomorrow. So I suppose I really ought to go back and do it now."

"We'll do it this afternoon, and I'll come with you," said Pooh.

"It isn't the sort of thing you can do in the afternoon," said Piglet quickly. "It's a very particular morning thing, that has to be done in the morning, and, if possible, between the hours of — What would you say the time was?"

"About twelve," said Winnie-the-Pooh, looking at the sun.

"Between, as I was saying, the hours of twelve

and twelve five. So, really, dear old Pooh, if you'll excuse me — *What's that?*"

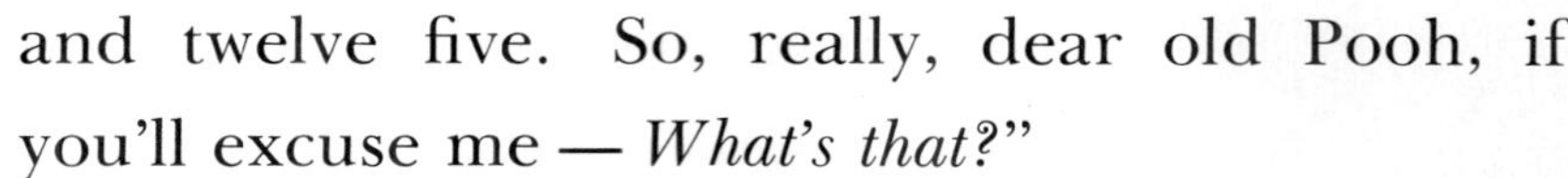

Pooh looked up at the sky, and then, as he heard the whistle again, he looked up into the branches of a big oak-tree, and then he saw a friend of his.

"It's Christopher Robin," he said.

"Ah, then you'll be all right," said Piglet.

"You'll be quite safe with *him*. Good-by," and he trotted off home as quickly as he could, very glad to be Out of All Danger again.

Christopher Robin came slowly down his tree.

"Silly old Bear," he said, "what *were* you doing? First you went round the spinney twice by yourself, and then Piglet ran after you and you went round again together, and then you were just going round a fourth time — "

"Wait a moment," said Winnie-the-Pooh, holding up his paw.

He sat down and thought, in the most thoughtful way he could think. Then he fitted his paw into one of the Tracks . . . and then he scratched his nose twice, and stood up.

"Yes," said Winnie-the-Pooh.

"I see now," said Winnie-the-Pooh.

"I have been Foolish and Deluded," said he, "and I am a Bear of No Brain at All."

"You're the Best Bear in All the World," said Christopher Robin soothingly.

"Am I?" said Pooh hopefully. And then he brightened up suddenly.

"Anyhow," he said, "it is nearly Luncheon Time."

So he went home for it.

108

AUTHOR

A. A. Milne began to write *Winnie-the-Pooh* as he watched his own son, Christopher Robin, at play. The real Christopher Robin had a stuffed bear named Winnie-the-Pooh, and Mr. Milne enjoyed writing about them. He also added other animals such as Piglet, Eeyore the donkey, and Kanga and Baby Roo. His four books about Christopher Robin and his animal friends are among the best-loved books in the world. *Winnie-the-Pooh* and *The House at Pooh Corner* are collections of stories. *When We Were Very Young* and *Now We Are Six* are books of poems.

A problem arose when these books first became famous. People became excited when they learned that A. A. Milne really had a young son named Christopher Robin. They began to write letters to the little boy, and some even came to the Milne house just to see him! Mr. Milne grew worried that his son would become spoiled by all this attention. The author became so upset about this that he decided not to write any more Christopher Robin books.

A. A. Milne was born in London in 1882. For many years, he was an assistant editor of *Punch,* a British humor magazine. He also wrote many plays, poems, and stories for grown-ups. But he is remembered most for his Christopher Robin books. Although Mr. Milne died in 1956, these books live on and are as popular as ever.

BOOKS TO ENJOY

THEY PUT ON MASKS *by Byrd Baylor*

Here is a colorful look at why and how American Indians have used masks, dances, and songs.

THE HAUNTED CHURCHBELL *by Barbara Byfield*

In a very unusual way, Sir Roger solves the mystery of why the churchbell rings every night at midnight.

THE GREAT CUSTARD PIE PANIC *by Scott Corbett*

Nick's mysterious adventure with Dr. Merlin, the magician, takes place in a bakery. A funny sequel to *Dr. Merlin's Magic Shop.*

GORILLA GORILLA *by Carol Fenner*

This outstanding science book is about a young gorilla of the African forest who is captured and taken to live in an American zoo.

FAVORITE FAIRY TALES TOLD IN DENMARK
by Virginia Haviland

This is one of the books in a popular series of easily-read tales. Each book has stories from a different country.

ANY ME I WANT TO BE *by Karla Kuskin*

Thirty animals and things describe themselves in these guessing poems that are written as riddles or puzzles.

THE DRAGON TAKES A WIFE *by Walter Dean Myers*

Mabel Mae and a dragon have a comical adventure in this mod fairy tale.

Expedition

All Except Sammy

by Gladys Yessayan Cretan

Everyone in Sammy Agabashian's family was musical — except Sammy.

Mama played the piano.

Brother Armen played the clarinet.

Sister Lucy played the cello.

Papa played the violin, and was the conductor of a whole symphony orchestra.

Sammy played baseball.

Sometimes the family gave a concert together. They played many kinds of music — sonatas and mazurkas and waltzes. Usually Papa and Armen did a duet especially written for violin and clarinet. Mama and Lucy always looked beautiful up on the stage in their long silk dresses.

Sammy sat in the audience and listened with the others.

When Armen played in his own recitals, or Lucy in hers, Sammy sat in front and clapped proudly along with Papa. Sometimes the people around them shouted "Bravo!" and Mama smiled happily.

Everyone said, "Such a talented family. All so musical."

Of course they meant everyone was talented but Sammy.

One day a man from the newspaper came to take a picture of these musical Agabashians. He grouped them all around the piano. Mama sat at the piano bench, with her music spread in front of her. Armen stood next to her with his clarinet, ready to play. Lucy sat with her cello, and Papa was a little to the side with his baton raised.

Then the newspaperman turned to Sammy. "And what do you play?" he asked.

"Baseball," said Sammy.

"That's a good game, but I can't put you in this picture," said the man. "This is a picture of a musical family."

So while the picture was taken, Sammy sat and watched.

Afterward he said to his mother, "I sure would like to be in the next family picture. What instrument could I learn?"

"We could use another violinist," his mother said. "We'll ask Papa to give you lessons."

Papa tried.

And Sammy tried.

But it never did sound right. In fact, it sounded horrible. When Sammy was playing, the cat scratched on the door to be let out, and the dog hid under the bed and howled. Even Sammy's best friend Jason quietly rolled his eyes and went home.

"Sammy," said his father, "even for a beginner this is terrible."

"Let's try the piano," said his mother, "and work on your rhythm."

For days and days they worked, and Sammy tried hard.

"Oh dear," said his sister Lucy.

"Something's wrong," said his brother Armen.

"*Hereek!* Enough!" said his father. "Mama, the boy has no rhythm. Absolutely no rhythm."

"Try again, Sammy," said his mother. "Listen

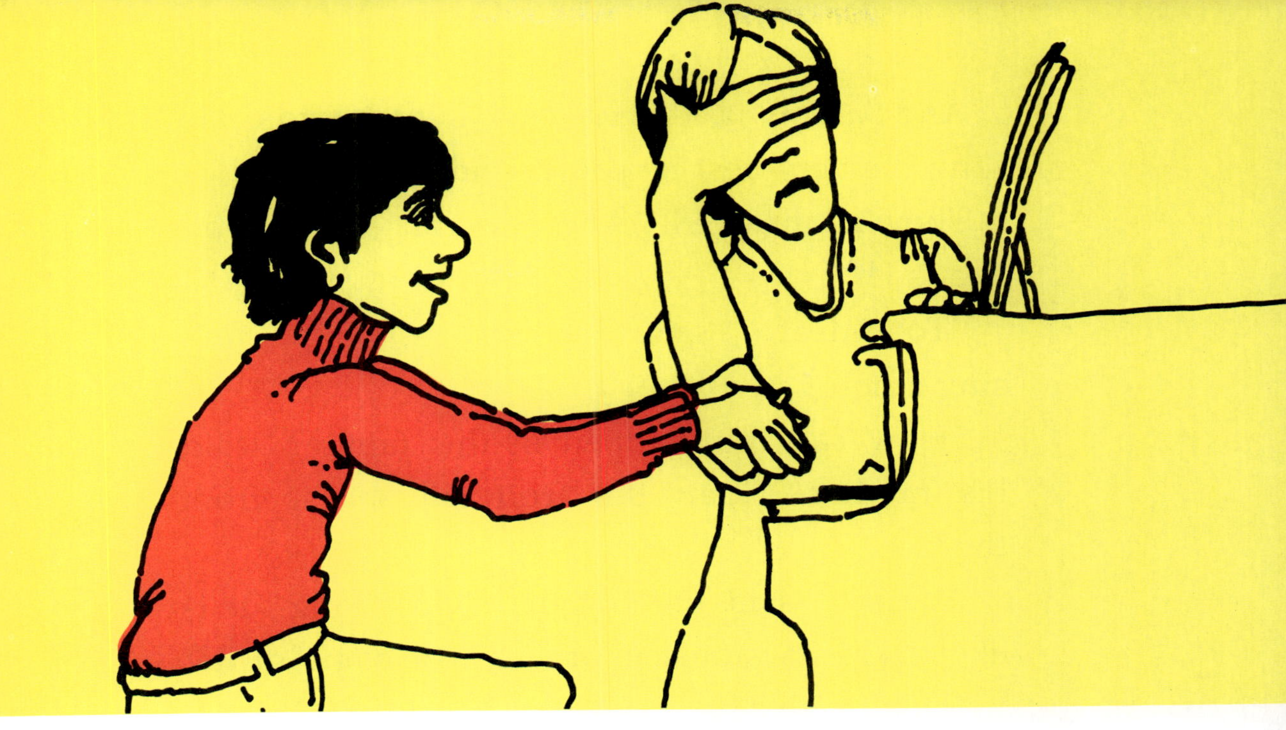

now. One-and-two-and — no, no, no. Sammy. Can't you hear the beat?"

She sat back and shook her head. *"Vagh!"* she said. "I'm afraid your father is right."

Then she had another thought. "Perhaps he will be our singer. And someday he will sing arias. Come, Sammy, what would you like to sing?"

"Take Me Out to the Ball Game," said Sammy happily.

"All right," said his mother, and she started to play it on the piano. "Come," she said. "Sing out, Sammy."

And Sammy tried. He knew all the words. He sang the very best he could, and loud.

They all listened. And they all shook their heads.

"Tone-deaf," said his father. "He can't sing a note."

"How can this happen in this family?" said his mother. "Can the fruit fall so far from the tree?"

"Mama," said his father, "stop trying. It is like baking a stone. Nothing will come of it."

"Don't feel bad, Sammy," said his sister. "It doesn't matter."

"Who's feeling bad?" said Sammy.

"Come on," said his brother. "Let's go out and play ball."

"Who cares about music anyway?" said Sammy. But Sammy really did want to be in a family picture.

After school the next day Sammy dashed home and ran upstairs to get his bat and mitt.

"There is a thunder in our house," said his mother.

"A thunder called Sammy," said his father, as Sammy rumbled down the stairs. "And look at that black cloud on his face. Why do you frown?"

"You'd frown too," said Sammy, "if you had to go to the museum."

"No," said his mother. "I often go, and it makes me happy. But why do you suddenly want to go to the museum?"

"Who wants to go?" said Sammy. "It's our homework. This week everybody has to go to the museum and find a favorite picture and tell about it."

"A good idea," said Papa.

"Listen," said Sammy. "I don't know anything about paintings. I don't even like them. How can I have a favorite?"

"Try," said his mother. "Slow down once and really look."

"One question," said his father. "Why the baseball bat?"

"Well," said Sammy, "I can't stay all day at the museum. I have baseball practice. And we're up for the championship."

He walked slowly to the museum, hitting each telephone pole with his bat. At the big gray building he stopped and wondered.

He hadn't ever gone in before.

He walked up the wide stone steps, and when he came to the great doorway he stopped again. He felt small.

When he stepped into the large center room with its statues and its curving stairs and its cool marble walls, he looked around slowly. His footsteps were very loud. A museum guard came up to him and told him he would have to check his bat at the front desk.

Then he climbed the stairs and wandered through the bright rooms. There were paintings of sunflowers, of children dressed in blue velvet, of dancers, pink on white.

Sammy shrugged and gave his mitt a punch.

"Too fancy," he said.

He passed a picture of an old castle, of a golden-haired family, of a bowl of fruit shining in the sunlight. He shook his head.

When he saw a sparkling picture of small boats sailing, he paused. That was better. But after a moment he walked on, wondering if he ever would find a real favorite.

He came back up the stairs, and that was when he saw the painting of a brilliantly dressed soldier sitting tall on a proud black horse.

"There!" he said. "There's a picture I could talk about." And he stopped and looked at it for a long time.

Across the quietness a voice said, "Hi, Sammy!" Sammy turned to see his friend Jason standing in front of a large picture of the sea.

"Hi!" said Sammy. "Find your picture?"

"I guess I like this one," said Jason. "Looks like a big storm. What about you?"

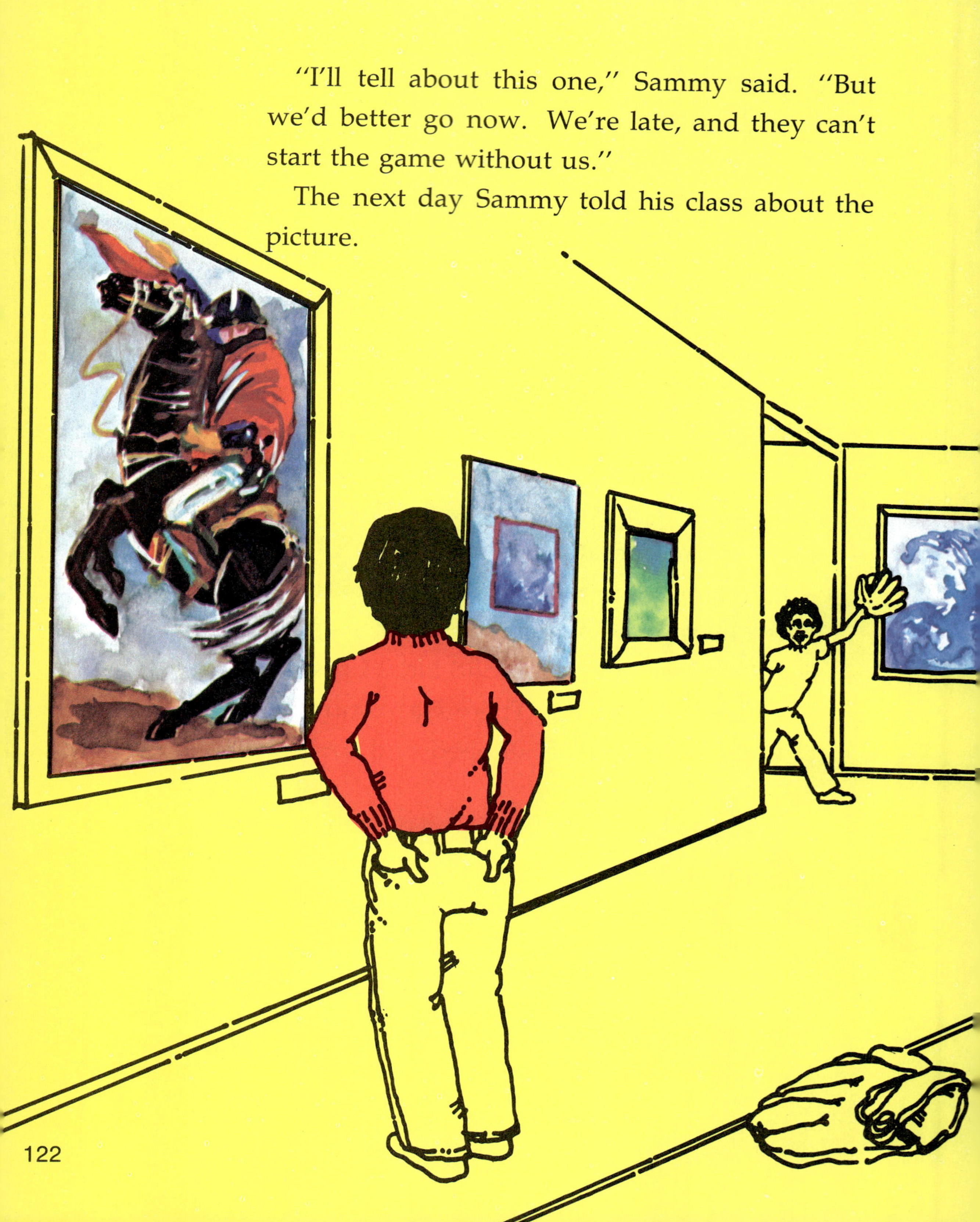

"I'll tell about this one," Sammy said. "But we'd better go now. We're late, and they can't start the game without us."

The next day Sammy told his class about the picture.

"And that horse could gallop, or trot, or run like the wind," Sammy said. Jason looked puzzled.

"Say!" he said later. "How could you tell how that horse could run?"

"You could see it in the picture!" said Sammy.

"Now look," said Jason. "I saw that picture, and I didn't see anything like that. And you even said that he had led a parade!"

"I could tell that partly from the ornaments he was wearing and partly from the proud way he held his head," Sammy answered. "Listen, if you don't believe me, we'll stop there today on the way to the ball park and I'll show you."

"All right," said Jason. "But man," he rolled his eyes, "gallop and trot?"

"Look," said Sammy after school, as they stood in front of the picture. "Look at the power in that horse. Look at his smooth muscles. You mean to tell me that horse can't run? And see how the soldier is holding the reins. He's sure of that horse. He knows he can do anything!"

After a long look, Jason shook his head. "That's a lot to tell from a painting," he said.

Sammy nodded. "It's a lot for someone to show, just with a little paint," he said.

Jason moved slowly on around the large room. But Sammy sat on a bench and kept looking at the same picture. Jason tried walking in a circle on his heels. He swung his mitt around and around and went downstairs for a drink of water. He whistled between his teeth. When he came back, Sammy still wasn't ready to go.

Jason scuffled his feet and waited and wait-ed. "Didn't you see enough?" he asked at last.

"Look at this," Sammy answered.

"Same old picture," said Jason.

"I've been looking at the soldier's cape," said Sammy. "It's supposed to be red."

"Sure is red," Jason said. "Bright red."

"Yes," said Sammy. "When I first saw it, I thought it was plain red. But I've really been looking at it. And I see that when you're close to it, part of it is orange, part of it is almost black, and part of it is white. But when you back away from it, it all comes out red."

Jason nodded. "I suppose an artist knows how to do that," he said.

"I'd like to know how to do it, too," Sammy said. "Look how he used the white and the dark to make it look like folds in the cape. Listen, that's harder to figure out than any puzzle. I'll have to come back tomorrow and look at that some more."

Jason groaned. "More?" he said.

But Sammy wasn't listening. He was pointing to a sign. It said there was a painting class for school children on Saturday mornings.

"Look!" Sammy said. "That's for me."

"Good," said Jason. "You can ask about that red. I sure was getting tired of studying it!"

Just As Tough As Playing Baseball

They walked down the wide steps and turned toward the ball field, and Jason thought of something else.

"Hey!" he said. "Sammy! What about Saturday practice?"

"I'll only be a little late," Sammy said. "I wouldn't miss that."

"Sure," said Jason. "But what about Tug Smith?"

"Look," said Sammy. "We decided in the tryouts. I'm first base, and he's my substitute."

"I know," said Jason. "But if you don't come on Saturdays . . . Oh, oh, look. He's already standing there as if he owns first base."

Across the field they could see Tug standing with one foot on either side of first base. When

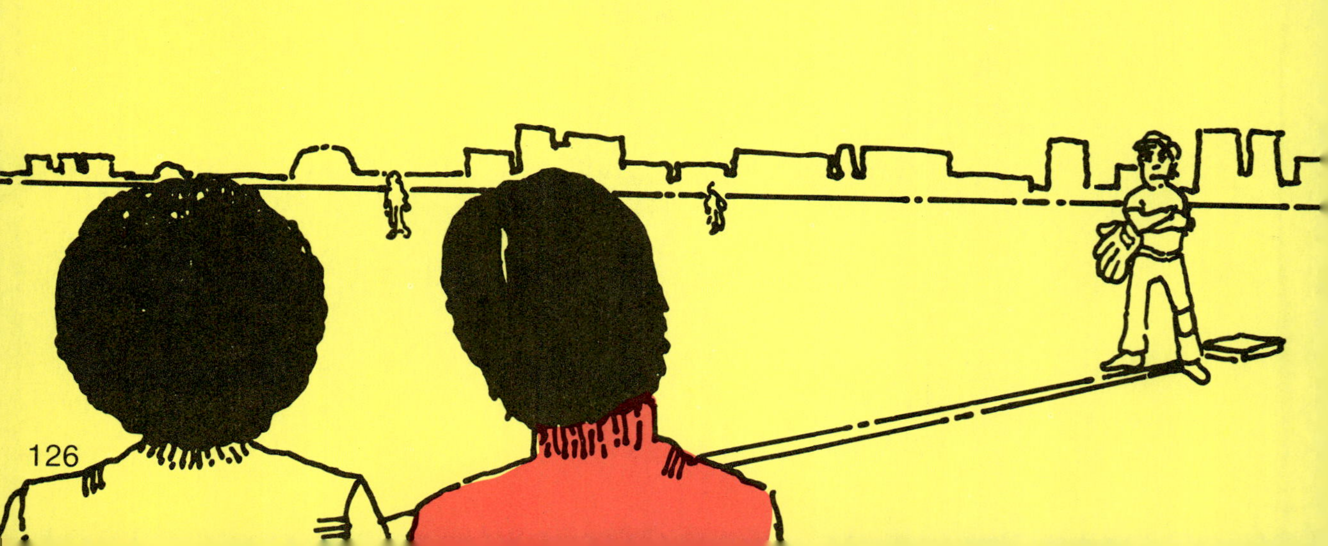

he saw them cutting across the field, he folded
his arms and pulled himself up tall.

"He's not planning to move," said Jason.

"Too bad," said Sammy. "Hi, Tug."

"Hi," said Tug. "They need someone in left
field."

"Good," said Sammy. "Then you can still
play."

"Not me," said Tug. "I'm first base."

"Since when?" said Sammy.

"Since you were late twice in a row."

"Listen," said Sammy. "I have to be late every
Saturday, and you're my sub, fair enough.
But I was chosen first base, and I'll be here as
fast as I can."

"How come you'll be late?" asked Tug.

Sammy hesitated. "I have to take a class."

"No school on Saturday," said Tug.

"I know," Sammy said. "This is a special class. Art. At the museum."

"Art?" hooted Tug. "Art? Hooo-eeee! Hey, fellas, he's going to be a painter."

"Cut it out!" said Sammy. "And get off that base."

"Make me get off, painter," laughed Tug. "Hooo-eeee!" And he doubled over.

Sammy stepped toward him with fists up and his head down.

"Fight! Fight!" said the pitcher.

"Get him! Get him!" said the catcher.

"I'll hold your things, Sammy," said Jason.

Tug laughed again and leaned down to slap his leg. Sammy jumped. Over they rolled. And over again. Arms and legs waved free, then were pinned down again. Under and over. Under again, and over they went. Dust flew. A shirt tore.

Suddenly Sammy was on top and had Tug pinned down. He wiped his forehead with his arm and he frowned down at Tug.

Everybody was quiet.

"Sammy," said Jason softly. "Don't hit him."

"Aw," said Sammy. "What's the matter with you guys? Why would I hurt him? He's even on our own team."

Then he looked back down at Tug.

"Listen," he said. "You're so smart. Can you paint a brown-black horse that looks like he can really run?"

Tug shook his head.

"Okay, and can you paint a storm at sea, or can you use orange and gray and white, and still have a cape look red?"

"No," said Tug.

"Neither can I," said Sammy. "But that's what I'm going to try to learn. And it's tough. Just as tough as playing baseball. See?"

Tug nodded, and as they both stood up and dusted themselves off, Sammy continued, "So I'll be a little late on Saturdays, and you can sub. Right?"

"Well," said Tug. He looked over to first base. Then he looked at all the faces around him, and back to Sammy. "Well, all right," he said.

So every Saturday, while Mama gave piano lessons downstairs, and Armen and Lucy practiced their instruments upstairs, and Papa went to symphony practice, Sammy went to the art class.

"What about the baseball team?" Papa asked as he walked one morning with Sammy toward the museum.

"I get there a little late," Sammy said. "But the fellows don't mind because I'm painting a poster for them. We'll be the only team with our own special colors and our own poster to put up whenever we're playing."

"They're lucky to have an artist on the team,"

said Papa. "Look at the trouble we have getting our program covers designed. And our posters for the front of the concert hall. *Agh!* Either they look like a grocery list or they look like circus posters! A musician needs a musical poster. Ah, well. Here's the museum. Learn well!"

When Jason arrived later, Sammy was sitting quietly in front of a picture of a little girl, looking, looking.

"Studying something new?" asked Jason.

"Blue," said Sammy. "This week I'm studying blue for a new painting I started. Look," he pointed, "look at that blue dress. Part green, and part black, but it all comes out blue."

"That's a fact," said Jason. "Never saw it that way before." He picked up Sammy's mitt and gave it a punch. "We get to use the big field today," he said. "Can you play late?"

"Sure," said Sammy. "There's no use going home early today, anyway. There's a man coming to take a picture of the family."

"You're in the family," said Jason.

"I know," said Sammy. "But he only wants the musicians in the family. All but me."

"Never mind, Sammy," said Jason. "Maybe you can't fiddle but you sure can draw."

"That's true," said Sammy. "I can draw. And I've been thinking. Why can't I design the program cover for their concert? And I'll bet I could plan a good poster. I could paint the instruments that they play . . . maybe in blue like in this picture. . ."

Sammy worked hard. He worked for days and days. Sometimes he painted at the museum, and sometimes at home. While he worked he would hum, "Take me out to the ball game. . ."

"*Vagh*," said Mama under her breath, when she heard him.

"Tone-deaf," said Papa, shaking his head.

But one day Armen called, "Look! Look at Sammy's poster!"

And Lucy said, "Why, this is better than any poster we've ever had."

And it was.

So this time when the newspaperman came,
he put Sammy right in the middle of the family,
holding his poster. And when the picture of
all the Agabashians appeared in the newspaper, they were called "An Artistic Family."

"Boy!" said Sammy. "Look at that! I finally
got in the picture."

"And why not?" said his father. "Must

everyone play an instrument? No. You are an
artist. And a good one!"

"Not only that," said Armen, "he's a good
ball player."

"Championship game tomorrow," said Lucy.

"We'll be there," said Papa Agabashian.
"All of us."

And the next day, there they were, sitting on
the bleachers, cheering the team. There were
all the talented Agabashians — except Sammy.

Sammy was at home plate, swinging his bat,
waiting for the pitch. When he felt the crack
of his bat against the ball he ran, ran, safe to
first base!

He heard the yells and the whistles of the crowd. He heard the clapping and shouting of Jason and the team. He heard his family calling, "Bravo!"

"Sounds like music to me!" he said.

AUTHOR

All Except Sammy was honored a few years ago by being chosen as a Junior Literary Guild book. The story was a natural one for Gladys Yessayan Cretan to write, for she herself is Armenian. When they were young, her parents came to the United States from Armenia. They settled in California where her father was a minister.

When Mrs. Cretan was a child, the family enjoyed many visitors in their home from the countries of the Near East. She learned to speak both Armenian and English as a child. When she grew up and did some traveling, she had many interesting experiences and warm receptions because she could speak the Armenian language.

Mrs. Cretan and her husband live in San Mateo, California, and they have two sons who are both interested in music. Other books with an Armenian background by Gladys Yessayan Cretan are *Because I Promised, A Gift from the Bride, Sunday for Sona,* and *Ten Brothers with Camels.* She is also the author of *Messy Sally, Lobo,* and *Runaway Habeeb.*

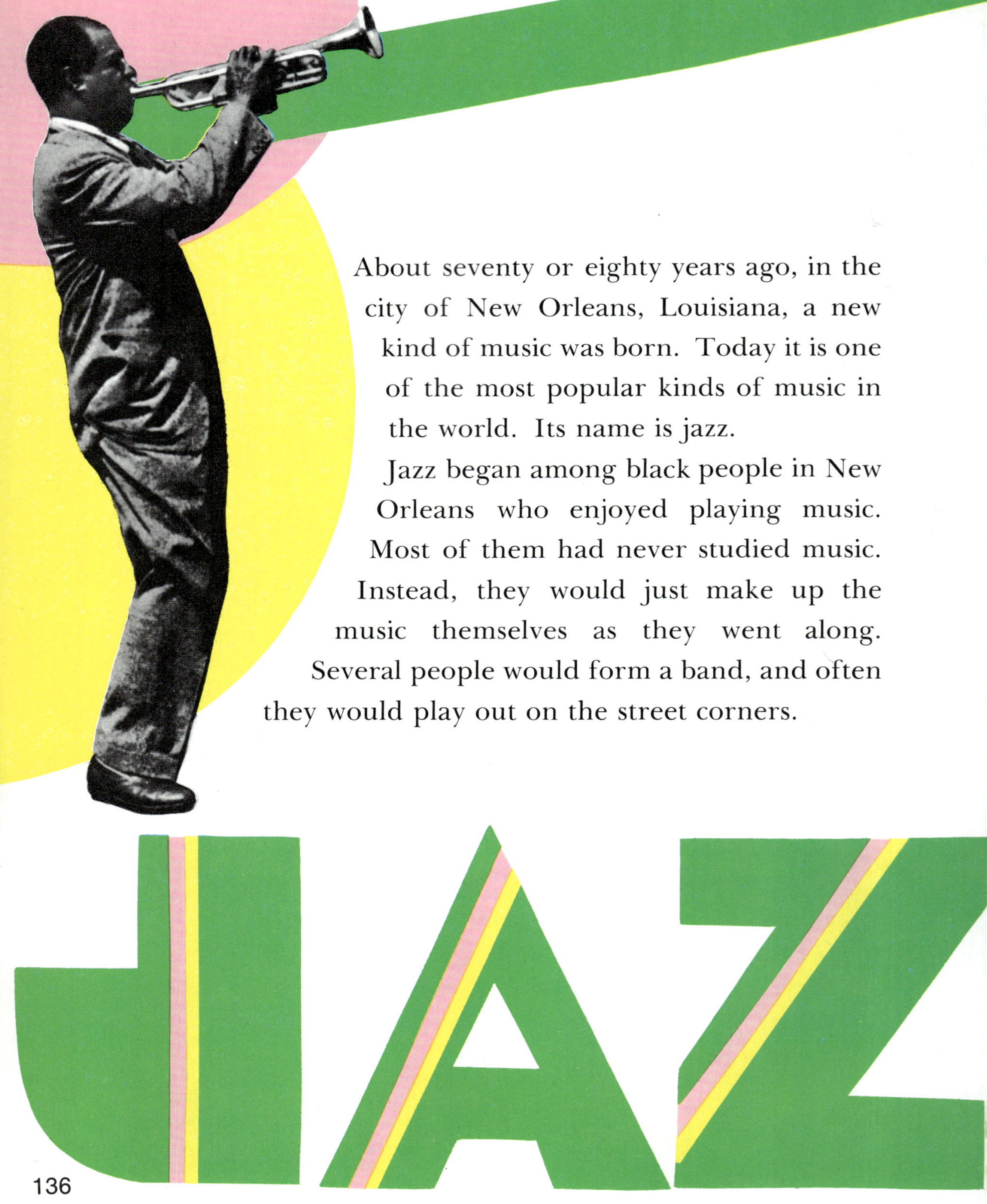

About seventy or eighty years ago, in the city of New Orleans, Louisiana, a new kind of music was born. Today it is one of the most popular kinds of music in the world. Its name is jazz.

Jazz began among black people in New Orleans who enjoyed playing music. Most of them had never studied music. Instead, they would just make up the music themselves as they went along. Several people would form a band, and often they would play out on the street corners.

His big chance came when King Oliver, a bandleader Louis had always respected, asked him to come to Chicago to be part of his band. Louis Armstrong soon became one of the most popular musicians of all time, playing his trumpet in almost every part of the world.

One of the great jazz composers was a man named Edward Kennedy ("Duke") Ellington. Duke was born in Washington, D.C. He loved to play the piano his own way, but he never liked to take piano lessons. He used to skip the lessons to

play ball with the other boys! But even at a young age, he had unusual talent.

In his early teens, Duke worked at a soda fountain. It was then that he composed his first piece of music, "The Soda Fountain Rag." After that he decided to become a musician.

Duke became well known when he and his band began playing at the Cotton Club in New York. During this time he composed much of his most famous music. Duke often got ideas from things he saw every day. Once he was watching a neon sign blink on and off. Suddenly he began to compose a piece in his head to the rhythm, and later he wrote it down. One of his most famous works, "Harlem Airshaft," came from listening to the sounds in a tall apartment house in the city.

Jazz is America's gift to the world of music. Louis Armstrong, Duke Ellington, and many others have made it a wonderful gift indeed.

If you would like to learn more about jazz and musicians like Duke Ellington (shown here), there are many excellent books you can read. Two of these are The First Book of Jazz by Langston Hughes and Journey Into Jazz by Nat Hentoff.

Skill

Lesson:

RECOGNIZING PARAGRAPH TOPICS

You know that almost everything you read is made up of groups of sentences that are called **paragraphs.** This arrangement of sentences in paragraphs can be a real help to you when you are reading to get some kind of information.

In starting to write a paragraph for a factual article, a good writer has in mind just one point or idea that he or she wants the paragraph to tell about. The writer makes the first sentence say something about that one thing. Then the writer makes each of the other sentences say something about that same thing. By the time the paragraph is finished, all the sentences in it say something about only one thing. We call that one thing the **topic** of the paragraph.

In the following paragraph, the sentences are numbered so that you can think about them easily later. As you read them now, try to decide what one thing all the sentences tell about.

1. Wherever people live, many of them have gardens. 2. Gardens may be big, or they may be small. 3. Some people have gardens mainly for beauty or fun. 4. They grow flowers like morning glories and roses in their gardens. 5. Other people use gardens mainly as a way to get fresh foods. 6. They grow things like melons, tomatoes, and squash.

Sentence 1 tells where *gardens* are found. Sentence 2 talks about the sizes of *gardens*. Sentence 3 tells one reason for having a *garden*. Sentence 4 tells what might be grown in a *garden* for that reason. Sentence 5 tells another reason for having a *garden*. Sentence 6 tells what might be grown in a *garden* for that reason. You can see that each sentence says something about the same thing, and that this one thing is gardens. That is why *gardens* is the topic of the paragraph.

To find out what the topic of a paragraph is, you must think what one thing all the sentences in that paragraph are talking about. Often you can do this quickly, right after you have read the paragraph just once. But sometimes you may have to study each sentence again to be sure.

When you do not know quickly what the topic of a paragraph is, do these things:

1. Read the first sentence again and think what it is talking about.
2. Do the same thing with each of the other sentences.
3. Then decide what one thing all the sentences are talking about. That one thing is the topic of the paragraph.

Whenever you read to get information, try to decide what the topics of the paragraphs are. Doing this can help you understand and remember what the paragraphs say.

Study the paragraph below and decide what its topic is.

In the early days of the United States, many people lived in cabins. The cabins were made from logs that were fitted together to make the walls. Other logs were split and used to make the roof. Usually a cabin was small and had just one or two rooms. But

it was a place in which a family could stay
warm and dry in the winter.

Which of the following topics is the topic of that
paragraph?

1. How cabin roofs are made
2. The cabins of early settlers
3. Building cabin walls
4. The size of log cabins

Discussion

Help your class answer these questions:

1. What is meant by the topic of a paragraph?

2. Which of the four topics is the topic of the paragraph
    you just read? Why is each of the other topics *not*
    the topic of the paragraph?

3. If you cannot decide quickly what the topic of a
    paragraph is, what can you do to find out what the
    topic is?

On your own

Read the following paragraph to yourself and decide what its topic is:

Bananas are eaten and liked by people in just about every part of the world. Bananas have in them most of the things people need to eat to stay healthy. They are grown wherever the weather is always hot and wet. More bananas are grown in South America than anywhere else. They grow in bunches on leafstalks that are so tall they look like trees. Bananas are picked when they are still green. They become yellow and ripe on the way to the stores where you buy them.

Checking your work

Help your class decide what the topic of that paragraph is. If you are asked to do so, explain how you knew that one of the following was *not* the topic:

1. Why people eat bananas
2. How bananas are grown
3. When bananas are picked
4. Where bananas are grown

METAPHOR

Morning is
a new sheet of paper
for you to write on.

Whatever you want to say,
all day,
until night
folds it up
and files it away.

The bright words and the dark words
are gone
until dawn
and a new day
to write on.

— EVE MERRIAM

Your Busy Brain

by Louise Greep McNamara and Ada Bassett Litchfield

Everybody says Maria is a brain. What do they mean? They mean Maria uses her brain well.

She uses her brain, as you use yours, to learn, to daydream, to ask questions, to solve problems, to make choices, and to make sense of the world around her.

Without a brain, Maria could do none of these things. And neither could you.

Put your hands on your head. You know where your brain is, but do you know what it looks like? If you could look inside your head, you would see a soft, wrinkled, pinkish-gray thing that fills most of the space in your skull. Feel the hard bones. Like a built-in crash helmet, your skull bones surround your brain and protect it.

Your brain knows many

Adapted from *Your Busy Brain* by Louise Greep McNamara and Ada Bassett Litchfield. Published by Little, Brown and Company.

149

things. When a fly is sitting on your nose, your brain knows it. Your brain tells the muscles in your arm to swat the fly. How does it do this?

Your brain is part of a network of nerves that runs down your spinal cord and all over your body. Your body uses this network of nerves to carry messages to and from your brain.

Message from nose to brain: A fly is sitting on me.

Message from brain to arm muscles: Swat it!

Like all the rest of you, your brain and nerves are made of cells. Some cells in your nerve network carry messages to the brain. Other nerve cells carry messages away from the brain. You might think of your brain as a giant control center, always receiving and sending messages.

Suppose you pick up a hot piece of pizza. Before the emergency message "HOT!" could go to your brain and come back to your hand, your fingers would be burned. A message from outside your body doesn't always go to your brain first. Sometimes there isn't time.

So that you won't be burned, this emergency message takes a shortcut to your spinal cord. A nerve in your spinal cord flashes back the order, "DROP IT!" In an emergency like this, your hand acts first. Your brain thinks about what might have happened, afterward. When you duck a ball that comes flying at your head, the same kind of emergency shortcut takes place. Can you think of other examples?

Your brain does more than receive and send messages. Like a big warehouse that stores many things, your brain stores information.

What do you remember? How long do you remember?

You have two kinds of memory: a short-time memory and a long-time memory. Things you don't need to remember, like a TV show you saw last night, are stored in your brain now, but may be forgotten in a few days. Things you need to remember, like your name and address and phone number, you repeat many times. Things you repeat many times usually become part of your long-time memory. Without a memory, you would have to learn the same things over and over. You would never have time to learn new things.

Your brain is made of three parts. The biggest

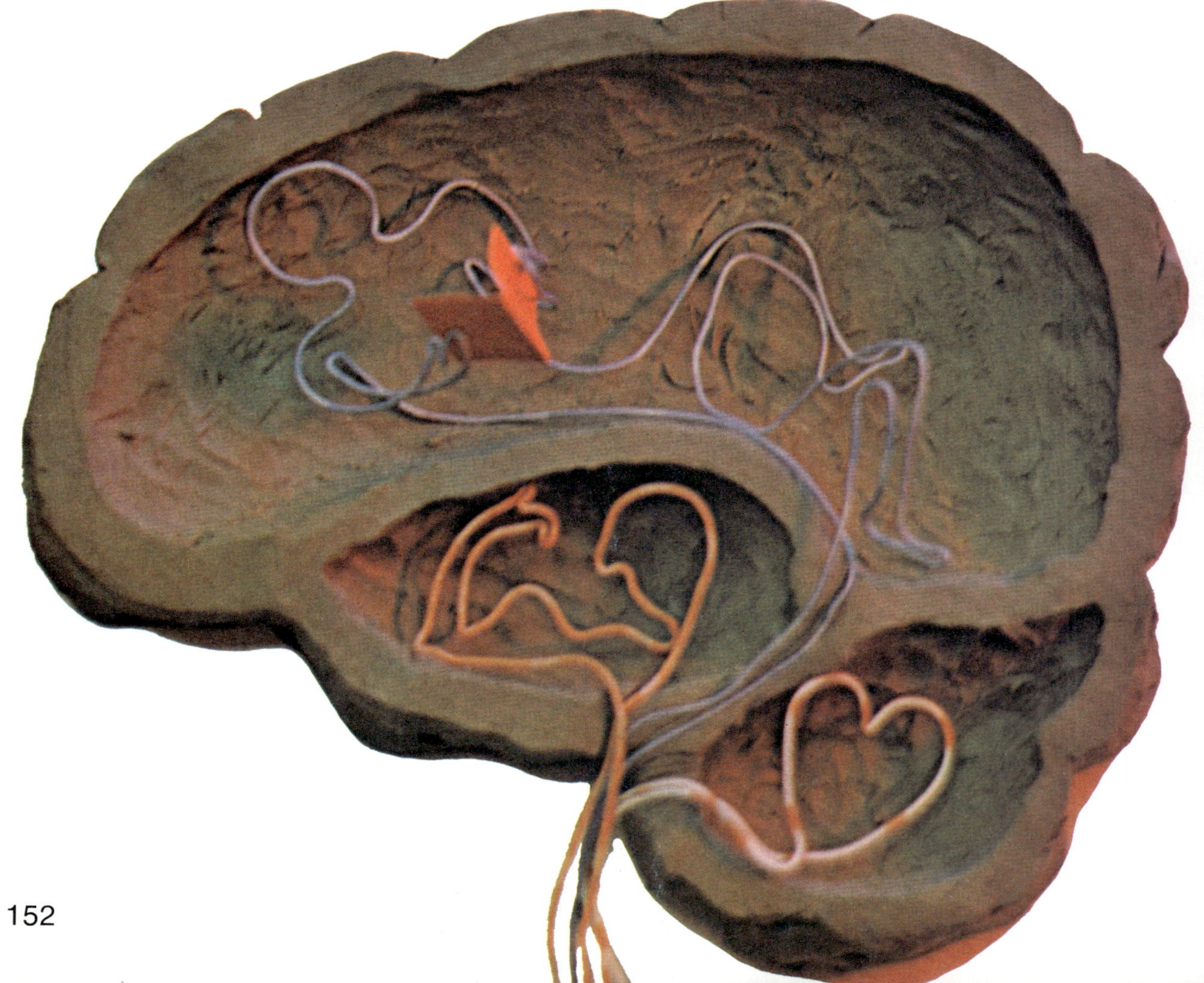

part, the upper brain, is at the top of your head. This is the part of your brain with which you think, and learn, and solve problems.

Underneath the big part of your brain is a smaller part, the middle brain. The middle brain keeps your muscles working together smoothly. Because of it, people can walk without stumbling, talk without mumbling, and draw without scribbling.

At the top of your spinal cord is the lower brain. It takes care of all the things you do without thinking, like breathing, swallowing, blinking, and digesting. It helps keep your heart beating and your blood moving.

Your brain never stops working. Even while you are sleeping, your heart is beating, your lungs are breathing, your food is digesting. And very often the thinking part of your brain is busy dreaming. Do you remember your dreams? What do you dream about?

Nobody knows for sure why you dream. But scientists who study dreaming know that you do dream every night, whether you remember your dreams or not.

Nobody knows for sure, either, just how you learn. Some things you learn by trying, and making mistakes, and trying again. Remember learning to ride a bike?

Sometimes at a fair or amusement park you will see a house made of mirrors and glass. You are supposed to go in one door, walk through the halls, and try to find your way out. It's fun, but it isn't easy. The walls of glass and mirrors mix you up. You may have to take many wrong turns before you find the right way out.

If you could look down on the fun house, this is what you would see.

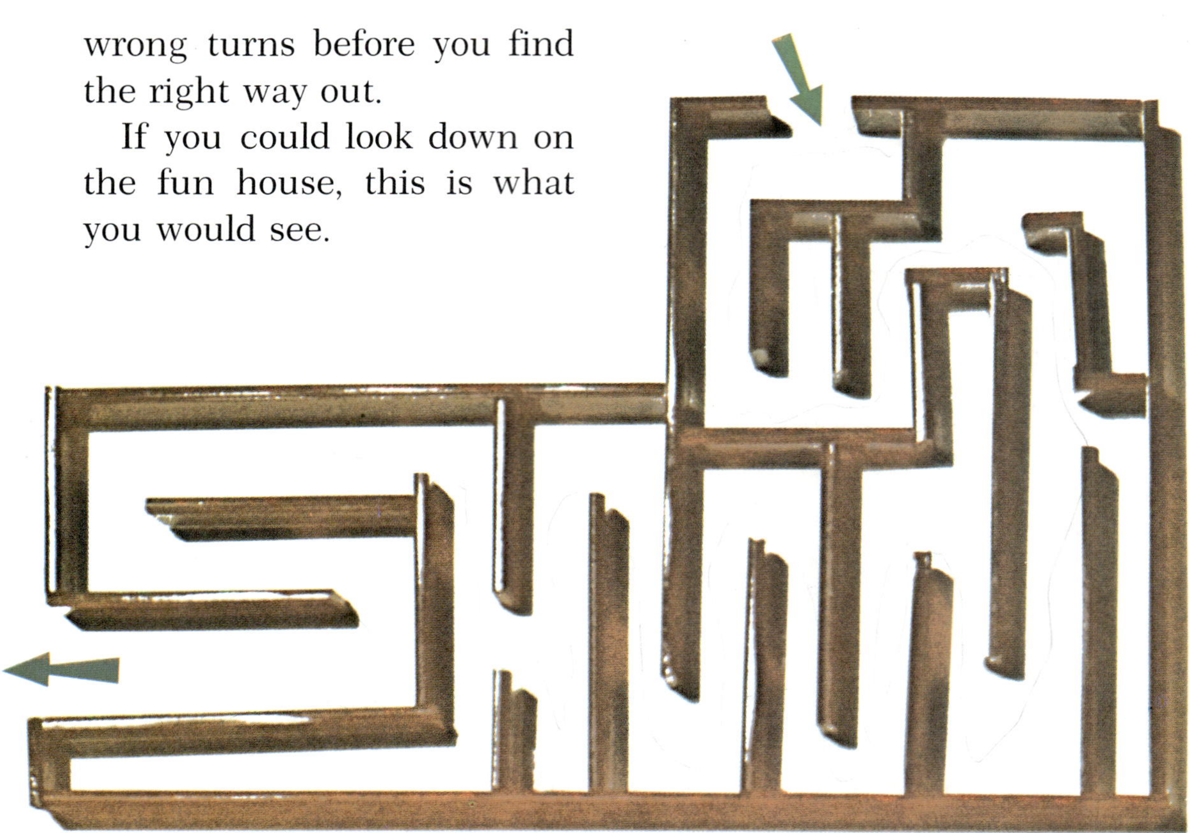

With your finger, start at the arrow and see if you can find the path you must take to get out again. Can you do it without mistakes the first time?

Try it again. It is easier the second time because some brain cells helped you remember the mistakes you made the first time you tried.

The human brain has created many wonderful things. But it is far more wonderful than anything it has ever created.

Every day you use your brain to learn what you want to learn, to do what you want to do, and to be what you want to be. It is always working for you — your own busy brain.

AUTHORS

Ada Bassett Litchfield started writing for fun when she was twelve, and she has been writing and working with books ever since. She has been a teacher and has worked in book publishing companies. At one time she also worked for a company that makes greeting cards. She and her husband, both fond of cats and gardening, live in Stoughton, Massachusetts.

Mrs. Litchfield was writing scripts for a TV series called *All About You* when she met Louise Greep Mc-Namara. Mrs. McNamara was the TV teacher for this series. The two women became friends and decided to write some books together to explain how different parts of the body work. Two of these books — *Your Busy Brain* and *Your Living Bones* — were honored by the National Science Teachers Association as two of the outstanding books of science for young people in 1973. Mrs. Litchfield and Mrs. McNamara have also written *Your Growing Cells*.

Louise Greep McNamara became a TV teacher after working several years in a regular classroom. She, her husband, and their three daughters live on the seashore of Massachusetts.

Besides working together on books, both women have written books on their own. Mrs. McNamara is the author of *Henry's Pennies*. Mrs. Litchfield has written *I Can, Can You?*, *The Good Morning Book*, *The Wonderful-Wonderful Book,* and *The Good-Night, Sleep-Tight Book.*

A RIDE ON HIGH

By CANDIDA PALMER

Tony awoke and remembered it was Saturday. Today he would ride the elevated to the game at his big cousin Charlie's school.

He listened for the rumble of the elevated trains passing back and forth on high tracks above his street. This morning he heard a wet, spattering noise as well. He jumped out of bed, ran to the window, and squeezed behind the window shade. Brr-r-r-snap! The shade flew up and flapped around the roller at the top.

"Oh, rain!" Tony groaned. Rain spoiled everything! "There'll be no game, so there'll be no ride on the el!"

A few minutes later, there was a knock at the door. It was Charlie.

"Will the rain stop?" Tony asked Charlie. Charlie was on the Roosevelt Junior High baseball lineup today.

"They haven't called off the game," Charlie said. "I'm going anyhow. There's practice first. Here . . ." He handed Tony two free passes for the game, for himself and for his best friend Chester. "And mind that you two little kids don't give me any trouble." Charlie put on his raincoat and raced out the door.

Tony watched at the window. By mid-morning the first watery sunshine sparkled on the shiny black street. He jingled the two quarters for his train fares in his pocket, just for luck. After lunch the ground was dry.

"Hurrah, we can ride the elevated!" Tony yelled. He ran all the way along his block and around the corner to Chester's house. Chester sat waiting on the steps.

"Have you got the passes and your money?" Chester demanded.

"Here, Chet, let's go!" Tony gave him one yellow pass and showed his two coins.

"I have an idea," Chester said on their way to the station at Fifty-second Street. "Together we have a dollar, right? Let's buy four tokens, two for our fares there and two to come back. Then there'll be change for candy."

At the newsstand under the stairs to the elevated, Chester studied the printed sign. "TOKENS: 4 for 90 cents," he read aloud.

They bought four shiny round brass tokens for the ride. The man gave them two nickels in change. Tony put his nickel into the slot of a candy machine. Out came a crunchy nut bar. Then Chester chose a caramel. They ran up the long iron stairs to the elevated station. There they each dropped one brass token into the slot of the turnstile. Click. The turnstile swung around and let them through to the train platform.

From the station Tony could see his house. Sparrows were splashing in a puddle on his roof. Today it was easy to find his window, because the shade was still tangled over the roller at the top!

Then Tony heard the train approach with a loud roar. It was rushing towards them like a silver monster. It stopped, and the doors slid open right where they stood. There were two empty seats together.

"Here we go!" Tony sang out. They were speeding along high above the playground now. The train stopped again. Tony counted the stops, four in all. He knew the stop for Roosevelt Junior High

Great!

came right after the narrow-pointed church steeple with the clock.

"I see Charlie's school," Tony was first to shout. The train slowed down and stopped. Quickly they stepped off. From the elevated platform, they looked down on the school buildings and the large playing field.

Tony pulled his pass out of his pocket. Whoops! Clink! His token jumped out with it. It rolled along its edge. He put his foot out, fast. He slipped. The token disappeared through a crack in the platform. He heard a faint, distant clink as it hit somewhere below.

"My token's lost!" Tony gasped with fright. "How'll I get home?" he wailed.

"We'll have to find it," Chester said, but he didn't sound hopeful. "Why don't you go down and look for it? Then if you don't find it, maybe you can find Charlie."

"Oh, he won't like that," Tony said quickly. "We could phone home . . ."

"Can't phone with tokens. Only money's good in phones," Chester answered. "You go down and take my last token. You'll need it to get back up. Maybe you'll just happen to see Charlie . . ."

A Long Ride Home

Tony took Chester's token, walked slowly through the exit turnstile, and down the long iron stairs. He looked for the token below the platform. He looked under parked cars. He sighed. He would have to find Charlie.

There were crowds at each gate and all along the fence. The band started playing "O Say Can You See?" The game was about to begin, and Charlie was probably already in the outfield.

A gruff voice demanded Tony's pass. Then he was pushed along in a slow stream of tall people up into the high bleachers. The baseball diamond looked very far away, especially the outfield. Was that tall player Charlie? He couldn't tell.

Tony watched two innings. A cold lump settled in his stomach when he remembered his lost token, and Chester up on the elevated station. He stood up and struggled out through the crowded row of seats. At last he found an exit. He ran all the way around the big playing field back to the elevated. He didn't stop running until he reached the turnstile at the top of the stairs. He dropped Chester's token into the slot. It was their last.

Chester's eyes were fixed on the distant playing field.

"Home run!" Chester shouted, jumping up and down.

"I'm back, Chet," Tony said in a small voice. "Didn't meet Charlie . . ."

"Never mind. I figured something out while you were down," Chester answered, smiling. "We can't cross the platform here and take the train back, not without paying new tokens. But when I went fishing with Uncle Ben, we rode on and on till there was no more track. I figure the train has to turn around. It's a long way, but we'll get a long ride home."

"Is it farther than the subway?" Tony asked.

"Much farther!"

"Is it past the Zoo?"

"Much farther!"

"Is it past the swimming pool in the park? I've never been farther than the park on the Fourth of July . . ."

"Still farther. It's ALL the way, and we have to come back ALL the way on that track over there," Chester explained. "You scared?"

Tony didn't want to sound scared. He could hear a train coming. He pulled himself up as tall as he could and held his breath. The roar of the train grew very loud. It stopped. There was only a moment to change his mind.

"Let's go, Chet," he said in a hoarse voice. They stepped aboard. Their train roared away.

Tony waited for the place where the trees and houses suddenly grew tall beside the track. Then, as if the ground swallowed them, track and all, the train rushed into the subway tunnel. There were stations underground, with lights and candy machines. Tony had always liked the subway ride best. Today it was so dark and spooky. He put his face close against the train window. All he saw was what looked like another lit-up train, just like theirs, going along beside them. A ghost train?

"Wish we'd come out," Tony whispered.

"Me, too," Chester agreed.

At last flashes of bright light shone between the
big steel uprights. Tony closed his eyes. When he
opened them, the train was climbing out of the
dark, spooky tunnel into the bright sunshine, up
to its elevated tracks. Now they could see where
they were going. Tony watched for the ZOO sign,
with the animal pictures. He also knew the park
stop. The train kept going and going. Rows of
chimneys were flashing by. Was there no end to

this big city? Tony hoped the train would remember to turn around!

They stopped again. Every single passenger
left the train and hurried off. Tony blinked his
eyes. A big smile was spreading over Chester's
face.

"I knew it! We're here!" Chester shouted and
ran to the door. He laughed and jumped up and
down. "Look, Tony! There comes a turned-
around train, all ready to take off for home!"

It was still empty. Tony and Chester chose the
very best seats. They were impatient for the motor
of the train to start up and the doors to close.

"We're off!" they yelled together. They
were going in the opposite direction now.
They were on their way home!

It didn't seem long before the elevated
train slowed down and the houses grew
tall beside it.

Whoosh! They roared through the magic subway tunnel again. Whoosh! Out they came!

"Roosevelt Junior High!" Chester called out. "See, everyone's gone home. Who do you reckon won the game?"

"Don't know . . . and don't care . . . This long ride home is best of all," Tony said. He laughed. "Chet, let's save quarters again and go for another ride. And it won't feel the least bit scary, 'cause it's a homecoming elevated, too!"

AUTHOR

The idea for *A Ride on High* came to Candida Palmer one Thanksgiving Day, as she and her family were riding the elevated in Philadelphia. They were riding to the end of the line in order to have Thanksgiving dinner with the Palmer grandparents. Crystal, Mrs. Palmer's daughter, was so excited with the long ride that another passenger turned to her and said, "Honey, is this the *first* time you've ever been on the elevated?" Mrs. Palmer then decided that children might enjoy reading a story about an elevated.

Mrs. Palmer came to the United States from New Zealand, where she grew up. She began to write stories for children when her own son and daughter, Logan and Crystal, started school. Her husband is a teacher in a college in Ohio. Mrs. Palmer has also written *Snowstorm Before Christmas.*

Beauty

by E-Yeh-Shure'

This poem was written about forty years ago
by a young American Indian girl.

Beauty is seen
In the sunlight,
The trees, the birds,
Corn growing and people working
Or dancing for their harvest.

Beauty is heard
In the night,
Wind sighing, rain falling,
Or a singer chanting
Anything in earnest.

Beauty is in yourself.
Good deeds, happy thoughts
That repeat themselves
In your dreams,
In your work,
And even in your rest.

TWO WEEKS OLD AND ON HIS OWN

by *VITALI BIANKI*

The little mouse was only two weeks old. He knew nothing about life. He didn't know how to search for food, hide from his enemies, or find shelter from wind and water. He didn't even know that he had enemies. But worst of all, he was unaware of the unseen dangers that were all around him.

One of those dangers was circling above him right now. A white gull had spied him. Soon Peek heard a whole flight of gulls screaming. They settled down on the water and paddled up alongside the little boat.

Peek was in trouble! What he didn't know was that a fish had seen the gulls and had come up to the surface. The fish was waiting for the gulls to tip the boat over, so that he could snap up the mouse in his sharp jaws. As the gulls came toward him, Peek closed his eyes.

Just then a fish hawk appeared overhead. Seeing the boat, the mouse, the gulls, and the waiting fish,

the hawk swooped down. With the tip of his wing he brushed the boat, turning it over. When the hawk flew off, he had the fish, and Peek was in the water.

Peek went down. Then he came up. And somewhere in between he learned to swim. Paddling furiously with all four feet, he swam to the wooden boat and clung to it with his teeth. A little later the boat crashed into some rocks and was flung upon a sandy shore. Peek leaped for the bushes.

He was soaked. Also he was very hungry. To find food, Peek had to leave his hiding place beneath the bush. As long as he could hear the screams of the gulls from the river, he was afraid to leave. So there he stayed, hungry and miserable. He was there in the afternoon. He was there in the evening. He was there when the sun went down and the birds went to roost. Everything became so quiet that he could hear nothing but water lapping on the shore. Only then, under cover of darkness, did he dare to leave his hiding place.

Even then he was cautious. Every few steps, he stopped and looked around him. There was no one. Growing bolder, he began to roll in the grass like a small dark ball, biting at the stems and leaves. No juice came from them. He began to tear them apart with his teeth. Suddenly the juice from a stalk came splashing all over his face. It was sweet and cool. Finishing that stalk, he searched for others. Peek was so busy searching for food that he did not notice anything going on around him.

Soon the moon came out. On all sides of him, Peek could hear faint rustlings and murmurs. Things were stirring in the bushes and in the grass.

The hungry little mouse went on eating. The tips of the stalk turned out to be delicious. Suddenly he heard a strange sound. Instantly his jaws stopped moving. His ears shot up. He listened.

"Bump bump." What a strange sound! "Bump bump." Something was hopping in the grass, straight in his direction. Peek thought of the bush and his hiding place. "Bump bump." Now the sound was behind him. "Bump bump." Now it was all around him, close by. Then there was a last "bump" right in

front of his nose. He found himself face to
face with a goggle-eyed little frog who stared
at him. Peek stared back. And there they sat,
staring at one another in amazement.

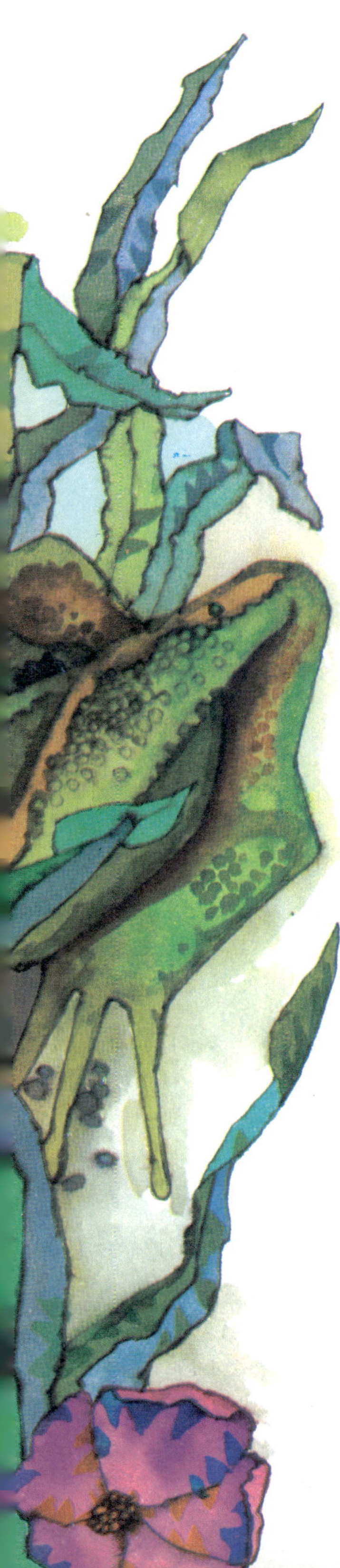

All around them the "bump bump" continued. Then there was a faint, swift, rustling sound in the grass. Peek, still staring at the frog, saw a silvery black snake slide up behind the frog. The snake struck. The frog disappeared into its mouth.

Peek fled.

He leaped for the high safety of a bush and crawled to the topmost limb. There, perched like a bird, he spent the rest of the night wide awake. All around him, until dawn, he could hear stirrings and rustlings in the grass.

In spite of the dangers around him, Peek was making progress. He had learned the secret of finding food. Now, if he could just find a way to protect himself from his enemies, he would be a happier mouse. If he had lived with other mice, this problem would not have been so serious. Mice look out for one another. When a field mouse senses danger, he makes a whistling sound, and the others run for safety.

But Peek was alone. If there were other mice in this dangerous world, he hadn't seen them. He could go look for them. Right away he started down from the bush where he had spent the night. Halfway down he turned quickly and ran back up again. He had remembered the snake.

Peek felt safer up there. For all he knew, the ground was covered with snakes, all of them waiting to pounce on him. If only he could travel above the ground! If he could just jump from bush to bush! If . . . And then Peek, looking around him, discovered his tail!

It was an amazing discovery, and a very useful one. His tail was long and could curl itself around twigs and small limbs. Trying it out, he curled his tail around a tiny branch and lowered himself to another. Then he leaped across to another bush, curled his tail around a limb, and swung through the air like a baby monkey to still another bush. No snake could get him now. For three straight nights, Peek traveled from bush to bush.

But finally the bushes ended, and one morning the little mouse looked out across a meadow. He was very hungry, and the meadow was filled with good things to eat. Boldly he climbed down from the bush in the bright sunshine and started digging for food. It was a dry meadow, and there seemed to be no snakes. But, though Peek didn't know it, there were other dangers just as deadly.

One of them was watching him right now.

It was a small bird hanging motionless in the air. Its wings were fluttering so rapidly that they did not

seem to be moving at all. This was a trembler, a bird about the size of a pigeon, only not so fat. Peek saw the trembler. It didn't seem dangerous. The bird just hovered in the air. Besides, the hungry little mouse had dug up some delicious beetle eggs and was sitting up on his hind legs, holding them in his forepaws and eating. The tiny white spot on Peek's breast shone bright against the brown earth.

It was the white spot which caught the sharp eyes of the trembler. Down he swooped, as silent as an arrow. Only then did Peek realize that the trembler was his enemy. But by then it was too late to run for the bushes. Peek flung himself flat against the ground and lay still, his heart pounding wildly.

The trembler missed him. Back into the sky the bird flashed, hovering motionlessly above. But now

no tiny white spot could be seen. Where it had been, there was only the color of brown earth. Peek's color blended perfectly with the ground. Though the bird looked and looked, it could see nothing. And yet, little Peek was lying there all the time, his heart hammering.

A moment later a green grasshopper jumped from the grass. The trembler darted, grabbed it, and flew away. Peek's enemy had gone.

The little mouse had learned two amazing things. One was that he had a most useful tail. He could also make himself invisible to even the sharpest eyes.

Peek had many other exciting adventures before he finally found a safe place to live. You can read about them in the book, Peek the Piper, *by Vitali Bianki.*

AUTHOR

Vitali Bianki was born in Russia. He has always been interested in nature and enjoys writing true-to-life animal stories such as *Peek the Piper.* He also writes folktales for boys and girls. Other books of Mr. Bianki's that you may enjoy are *Galinka, the Wild Goose* and *How I Wanted to Pour Salt on a Rabbit's Tail and Other Stories.*

Skill
Lesson:

GETTING HELP FROM COMMAS

You know that a **period** (.) usually says, "Come to a full stop here before you go on to the next sentence." You also know that a **question mark** (?) at the end of a sentence tells you to read that sentence as if you were asking a question. And you know that an **exclamation mark** (!) tells you that the word or words before it were said loudly or with strong feeling. We call such marks **punctuation marks.** They tell you something about how a sentence would sound if you heard someone saying it.

A **comma** (,) is another punctuation mark that you will often see in your reading. A comma usually says, "Slow down and pause slightly here before you go on to the next word." Doing that whenever you see a comma can help you in your reading.

As you read Sentence 1 below, see if you can decide what Bobby said he'd had to eat at a friend's house.

1. Bobby said he'd eaten fruit salad cheese biscuits beef pie applesauce cake nuts and lemonade.

Did Bobby have fruit and salad, or fruit salad? Did he have cheese and biscuits, or cheese biscuits? Did he have beef and pie, or beef pie? Did he have applesauce and cake, or applesauce cake? You can't tell, can you?

Read Sentence 2 below, and see if the added commas help you know quickly just what Bobby had to eat.

2. Bobby said he'd eaten fruit salad, cheese biscuits, beef pie, applesauce, cake, nuts, and lemonade.

Now you can see that Bobby had seven different things to eat or drink.

If you said that sentence aloud to tell someone what Bobby had eaten, would you make a pause between *fruit* and *salad?* Of course not! What would you do to make it clear that he'd had applesauce and cake instead of a special kind of cake called applesauce cake? You'd make a little pause between the words *applesauce* and *cake,* wouldn't you? You'd make a little pause wherever there is a comma in that sentence. Those commas stand for the little pauses or hesitations you would make in saying that sentence.

You can see that noticing those commas and thinking a little pause for each one helps you understand the sentence. Doing that will let you know what things Bobby had and will help you keep those things apart in your mind. Often you will find such lists of things, people, or ideas in sentences. When you do, just think a little pause for each comma. Then you will know what the different things are.

As you read Sentence 3 below, see if you can tell whether Terry is a boy, a girl, or a pet.

3. I took Terry to the park.

You have no idea who Terry is, do you? The speaker, though, could tell you who Terry is by adding another sentence, like this:

4. Terry is my younger brother.

Or he could have said this sentence in the first place:

5. I took Terry, my younger brother, to the park.

By adding the words "my younger brother" to Sentence 3, the speaker could make one sentence do

the job of two. Notice that when those words are added, a comma is placed before and after them to tell the reader to make a little pause for each one so that he will know that those words are about Terry.

When a group of words is set off from the rest of a sentence by a comma or a pair of commas, those words very often tell something special about the naming word that comes just before or just after them. Only one comma is needed, of course, when the group of words comes at the beginning or end of a sentence:

6. A slow-moving and good-natured animal, the porcupine is well protected by thousands of sharp spines loosely fixed to its skin.

7. One of the fastest runners of all animals is the ostrich, the largest bird known today.

Notice that if the group of words set off by commas had been left out, you would still have a perfectly good sentence. You can see that you have no trouble understanding those sentences if you just think a little pause when you come to each comma.

As you read Sentence 8 below, think what the word between the commas does:

8. Dad will give us a ride, Jim, if you're ready now.

Is the word *Jim* the name of one person in a list of names of people? Does the word *Jim* tell something

special about the word *ride?* No, it names the person to whom someone is talking, doesn't it? When you see a name of someone or something set off from the rest of a sentence by a comma or a pair of commas, remember that the name may be telling you who is being spoken to. Usually, such a name and the words used with it will appear within **quotation marks** (" ") to show that someone is talking.

Decide who is being spoken to in these sentences:

9. "Ken, can you help me?" asked Mother.

10. "Where are you going, Pete?" asked Bill.

Now look at the next two sentences. They are just alike except that one has two commas and the other has only one. See if you can decide what the difference in meaning is between the two sentences. Be sure to pause a bit when you come to a comma.

11. Alice, the girl next door, is the same age as you.

12. Alice, the girl next door is the same age as you.

Discussion

Help your class answer these questions:

1. What do we call marks like periods, question marks, exclamation marks, and commas? How can such marks help you in reading?

2. Why is Sentence 2 easier to read than Sentence 1? Where should the commas have been if Bobby had had fruit and salad, cheese and biscuits, beef and pie, and applesauce?

3. Sometimes a group of words coming next to a naming word is set off from the rest of the sentence by a comma or a pair of commas. What does such a group of words often do? What two sentences could you easily make out of Sentence 6? Out of Sentence 7?

4. Sometimes a person's name is not in a list of names but is set off from the rest of a sentence by a comma or a pair of commas. Why? Who was being spoken to in Sentence 9? In Sentence 10? What are quotation marks?

5. What is the difference in meaning between Sentences 11 and 12?

On your own

As you read the paragraph that follows, remember to think a little pause for every comma. Decide why each word or group of words set off by a comma or a pair of commas was set off that way from the rest of the sentence.

Mark wanted a baseball, glove, and bat for his birthday. His mother let him have a party and invite five of his friends, all of whom were boys that lived nearby and were in his class at school. He was disappointed when Dick, his best friend, could not come. Jim, Frank, Larry, and Tom arrived right on time. The boys played games that Mrs. Blake, Mark's mother, had planned. Each one of the guests received a prize, a model airplane kit. The boys enjoyed birthday cake, ice cream, and chocolate milk. "It's time to open your presents, Mark," said Mrs. Blake when the boys had finished eating. Usually a very calm boy, Mark jumped up and down with delight when he found a ball, glove, and bat in the package from his parents. Mark thought it really was a perfect birthday, just about the best he could possibly have had!

Checking your work

If you are asked to do so, read one of the sentences in the paragraph above, and explain how the commas helped you to understand the meaning.

Annie and her younger brother Stevie lived with their grandmother in an apartment house near the railroad. From the roof of the building they could see the trains passing. Stevie always seemed to be in trouble. But he had become very fond of his teacher, Miss Stover, and her dog Skipper. Miss Stover seemed to know how to make Stevie behave.

Then Miss Stover had to leave the city for a while because her mother was ill. Stevie was quite upset about this. He had begun to go around with some boys who were getting into more trouble. Annie became especially worried when she heard that the boys were throwing rocks at passing trains. Annie didn't want her grandmother to find out. She knew she was going to have to do something.

In this section from Eleanor Clymer's book, My Brother Stevie, Annie tells her own story.

I heard Stevie and his friends scrabbling around in the trash and saying, "I got a good one!" They were putting things in their pockets, pieces of glass and stuff. And then they ran to the elevator and banged the door shut.

I thought, "I bet I know where they're going. They are going to the roof, and fire rocks and things at the trains." I wondered if I should run after them, or tell Grandma, or the superintendent, or the guard, or just forget it.

If the guard caught them, they would be in trouble for sure. I thought I'd better follow them. So I ran to the other elevator, but it took a long time coming. At last it did, and I ran to the roof.

I didn't see the boys. I thought maybe they changed their minds, but then a train came along, all lit up like a string of beads, and there was a tinkling crash, and I could see people in the train jumping up and down.

Then I heard feet running, and two men shouting, "Come here, you little rats!" And there was the sound of a smack, and somebody yelling, "Ow! I didn't do it."

Then each man was dragging a kid off by the back of the neck. I couldn't see if Stevie was one of them. But I went down to the apartment. I was shivering and shaking as much as if I had done something, and I hoped I wouldn't see Grandma. But luckily it was Friday night and she had gone to church.

I felt awfully thirsty and I was just taking a drink of water when the door opened, and Stevie ran in. He was breathing awful hard and he flopped down in a chair.

I said, "Are you sick?"

He said, "No, I was playing."

I thought, "I'm not hiding this any more." I said to him, "Stevie, I know where you were. And if you don't do what I say, I'm going to tell the guards and the police, and you will go to reform school and never get out."

If he hadn't been so young, he would have

known I would never really tell the police.
But he was scared, and he believed me. So he
said, "What do you want me to do?"

I said, "Tomorrow is Saturday, and from now
till Monday you are not going to go out of this
house unless I say you can."

He said, "All right, I wasn't going out anyhow," bold as anything.

So I gave him some supper that Grandma had
left, and said, "You eat that now and go to
bed, and I'll decide later what you have to do
next." And he did.

And I sat in the kitchen and thought, "I fooled him into it this time, but I have to make a plan, and it better be good."

I sat and thought and thought, and ate a piece of bread, and then I got an idea. I would take Stevie to see Miss Stover and Skipper. Miss Stover was still in Hacketsville taking care of her sick mother. I didn't know how I would get us there, but somehow I would.

I went into Stevie's room and he was in bed with his clothes on, looking at a comic. He wouldn't look at me.

I said, "I'm going out for a while, but you stay here. If Grandma comes, say I went to Betty's and I'll be right back. Did you hear me?"

He didn't answer. He was mad at me.

I said, "Did you *hear* me? Answer me when I talk to you."

He grumbled something and I went out. I took my pocketbook and all the money I had. It was about three dollars. It was what I had been saving for new shoes, but I would have to start all over again. I went to Betty's and asked her to lend me some money. I said it was very important, but not to ask me what it was, be-cause it was to keep out of trouble, and it would be better if she didn't know. So she took every cent she had, about four dollars, and said she wasn't going to the show tomorrow anyhow. Betty is a real good friend.

Then I went to the station. I walked all the way so as not to waste any money, because I didn't know how much I would need. It was dark, and I was pretty scared, but nobody bothered me. When I got there, I said to the man, "Are there any trains that go to Hacketsville?" and he said, "Tonight?" and I said, "No, tomorrow."

He said yes, and I said, "How much for a ticket?"

He told me it was three dollars round trip, and I got two tickets. Then I went home. I only had about a dollar left but I took a bus, and when I got off the bus, I ran because it was late.

Grandma was home by then, and Stevie was asleep. Grandma didn't ask me any questions. I thought of what I was going to do, and felt mean, not telling her. But I thought, "I can't tell her. She wouldn't understand."

But the real reason was she would say it was crazy, and I knew that was true, and that's why I was scared. So I drank some milk and went to bed.

The next day was Saturday, and it was a nice sunny day. I got up early and said to Grandma, "Is the laundry ready?"

She said, "What's your hurry? You aren't even dressed."

So I said, "I want to take Stevie to the show."

She said, "You do? What's the matter? Can't you go with your own friends?"

I said, "Sure, but I thought it would keep him out of mischief."

She looked surprised, but she said all right.

She went and got all the wash. I thought, "I'd better take Stevie with me and not let him out of my sight." So I went in his room and said, "Come on, get up. We have to do the wash. You get up and help me, and I've got a surprise for you."

"What is it?" he wanted to know.

I said, "I'm going to the show and you can come. I have some money."

He said, "What show?" And I said, "Downtown. But you have to help me or I won't get done in time." So then he got up and we went out and did the wash.

When we came home I said to Stevie, "Now you wash your face and put on your good pants, because I'm not taking you if you look like a tramp."

Then I made some sandwiches and put them in a bag, and put on my good dress, and said good-by to Grandma. She gave me a funny look and said, "Wait." She took her pocketbook and took out two dollars and said, "Here."

I said, "Thanks, Grandma," and wanted to kiss her because I knew she couldn't afford it, and I felt as if I was leaving her forever. But she would have thought I was crazy, so I didn't.

Stevie and I went down in the elevator and I
started walking, and he said, "Hey, where
are you going? That's not the way to the subway." And I said, "This is the real surprise."

I showed him the tickets and said, "We're
not going downtown to the show. We're going
on a train to see Skipper and Miss Stover."

He started to yell, "You're nuts!" and was
going to run away from me, but I grabbed him
and held on tight and said, "Come on, we
can do it. I never was on a train, and I always
wanted to go. But I thought it wasn't fair to
go without you. So come on, because you
learned about trains at school and you know
more about it than me."

Well, he calmed down and right away he proved he did know more about it. He said, "Have you got a timetable?"

I said, "No, I didn't even think of it. I thought they just ran every few minutes, like the subway."

And he said, "They don't run all the time, only maybe every couple of hours. We'd better take the bus because we might just miss one."

So we jumped on a bus, and it crawled so slow I thought I would scream. It stopped for every red light, and then it stopped at every corner for people to get on and off, and a taxi would get in the way, and while we waited the light would turn red. But at last it got there, and we jumped off and ran like crazy, and I said to a man, "When is the next train to Hacketsville?"

He said, "One is coming in right now. Run and you might get it."

Well, it was a good thing Stevie had been in the station before with his class from school, because he knew just where to run. There was a train making a noise like it was all ready to go. We jumped in and a man outside waved his arm, and it started.

We sat down all out of breath. Stevie sat next
to the window, and I could see that he was real
excited. He'd been in the train before, but not
moving, and here it was really going.

It went faster and faster, and we were going
past houses and streets. You could sit there
and look right into people's windows. It felt
funny, as if we were on the other side of a
mirror. I thought, "I could be the person in
that window, watching the people in the train
going some place where I never went, and
seeing things that I never would see — and I
might feel like throwing a rock at them." I
looked at Stevie and wondered if he was thinking
the same thing.

We went over a bridge across a river and out of the city limits. Then a man came along and said, "Tickets, please."

"This is it," I thought. He might say no kids allowed without grownups and make us get off, and where would we be?

I had an idea. I gave Stevie the tickets and said, "Here, you hand them out." Stevie still looked real cute when he was good, and the man might be nice to him.

And he was. He winked at Stevie and said, "Yes, *sir*!" He tore them in half and gave Stevie back the other half and said, "Here you are, sir. Don't lose them." And he went on by. Boy, that was a relief.

Then I wondered how we would know when to get off, but Stevie said the conductor would call out the stations. And sure enough he did, every time we came to one. At last I heard him shout, "Hacketsville, the next station stop!"

We stood up and I grabbed my pocketbook and my paper bag, and the train slowed down and we got off. Then all the people who had come to meet somebody started hugging and kissing and saying, "It's good to see you." And the

train started up and went faster and faster
till it was gone. All the people got in their
cars and went away, and there we were alone.

My, it was quiet. I never heard anything so
quiet.

Then Stevie said, "How are we going to find
Skipper?" And I thought to myself, "That's a
good question. Here it is the middle of the
afternoon and not a living soul to ask."

Finally I said, "Maybe there's a store around
here. They might have a phone." So we walked
up a hill, and there were some houses on a

street, and a few stores. That made me feel a little better. At least there were some people in this place. So I said, "Come on." We found a phone booth out in the street, with a phone book in it, a little one. I grabbed it and looked for Miss Mary Stover. She wasn't there.

Now what? I was beginning to think Stevie was right and I *was* nuts, coming out here without letting her know. Stevie stood there looking at me, and waiting for me to do something, and I felt scared.

"There's a drugstore," I said. "Let's get a soda."

We went in and asked for two orange sodas. The man looked at us as if he was wondering who we were and where we came from, but he gave us the sodas and we drank them. Then I said, "Mister, could you tell us where R.F.D. 1 is?"

He stared at me as if I was talking Chinese.

I said, "We came to see Miss Mary Stover. She lives in Hacketsville, New York. The number is R.F.D. 1."

He said, "R.F.D. 1 isn't a number. It's a post office address."

I said, "Oh. Well, how can I find her?"

He said, "Did you look in the phone book?"

"Yes, but she isn't in there."

He said, "Does she live with somebody?"

"Yes, her mother."

He looked puzzled. "Can't help you," he said. "Where did you kids come from?"

I didn't want to say. I said, "Oh, we just came to visit."

The man said, "Too bad the post office is closed. Ernie might know."

I was getting awfully tired. I wished Stevie and I could just get back on the train and go home. At least, at home when they give you an address, it means something. I could see Stevie was tired, too. He sat on his stool all sort of droopy. I thought, "In a minute he'll fall off."

Suddenly the man pointed out the door and said, "There's Ernie now!"

We looked and there was a letter carrier. He had on a blue uniform and was getting out of a red, white, and blue truck. At least *that* was the same out here.

The drugstore man yelled, "Hey, Ernie! Come on in here!" The letter carrier came in. The man said, "Ernie, you know a Miss Mary Stover out Spring Hill way?"

I held my breath. Then I let it out again. Ernie was nodding his head "yes." He said, "Sure, that's one of Mrs. Carter's girls."

I shook my head. I was ready to cry. I said, "She's not a girl. She's a lady. A teacher."

"That's right," said Ernie. "Why do you want to know?"

The drugstore man said, "These kids came to see her."

Ernie said, "Well, you could phone her, see if she's there. I heard she was back. Mrs. Carter's sick."

The drugstore man looked in the book again
under Carter, and this time he found a number.
He dialed it. I held my breath again. Then
I heard him talking.

"Miss Mary Stover? This is the drugstore
in town. There's two kids here to see you.
I'll let you talk to the girl." He called me over
and said, "Here you are."

And I took the phone and said, "Miss Stover?"
My voice was shaking so much I was sure she
couldn't hear me.

Then I heard her voice, all steady and natural, just the way she always sounded. She said, "Hello! Who is it?"

I said, "This is Annie Jenner, and I'm here with Stevie. Do you remember us?"

She said, "Of course, Annie, but how in the world did you get there?"

"We came on the train, and now we're in the drugstore. I thought we could find you and just say hello, but I don't know where you are —" and my voice started shaking again.

She said, "Let me talk to the man again, please."

The man got on the phone and talked a little, and then he hung up and said to us, "It's all right. She said to put you kids in a taxi and send you out there."

Ernie and the other people in the store were all listening by this time, and when he said that about the taxi they all smiled, and nodded their heads as if they were glad, and I thought, "They're nice people."

Then Ernie said to the drugstore man, "I'll take them over to the taxi." So we went with him. I was hoping I'd have enough money to pay for the taxi.

A Statement by Stevie

We started out, and what a ride! Up a hill past some big fancy houses, some woods, and a field with horses.

Stevie yelled, "Look at the horses!"

Then we came to some smaller houses, with lots of kids playing around, and wash hanging out, not fancy at all. The taxi seemed to be slowing down, and I thought, "This can't be it!" But suddenly the taxi stopped in front of one of the houses, and the man said, "Here we are!"

Suddenly Stevie opened the door and jumped out. Something big and brown came running at him barking like crazy, and Stevie grabbed it and they rolled on the ground. It was like an explosion, shouting and barking and rolling

around. What a greeting! People came running out, and you never saw such a commotion in your life.

I grabbed Stevie up off the ground, but Skipper, the dog, kept jumping up and licking us both. Then I saw Miss Stover, and she held out her arms to Stevie and he ran into them and hugged her.

Then she kissed me too, and I almost cried but I didn't. I wished I could be as young as Stevie and run into her arms that way.

She paid the taxi man and said, "Thanks very much," and I could hardly believe it — it was only a dollar. He drove away grinning and waving his arm out the window. I never saw a taxi man do that before.

Then Miss Stover said, "Well, this is a wonderful surprise!" And I had a good look at her. She didn't look like a teacher at all. She just looked like any grown-up girl. She had on pants and a sweater, and her hair in a ponytail, and no lipstick.

She said, "I'm sorry I didn't know you were coming, or I would have been down to meet you."

Then I saw that there was a bunch of kids

hanging around the side of the house staring at us, and Miss Stover said, "Come here, children. I want you to meet two friends from the city. This is Stevie and this is Annie. You go and play now, and pretty soon I'll call you to a party."

Then she took me inside and said, "I'll introduce you to my mother, but we won't stay long because she has been sick and isn't very strong yet." She took me into a bedroom, and there was a lady in bed, propped up against the pillows.

Miss Stover said, "Mom, this is Annie Jenner. She brought her little brother out to see us from the city. Don't you think that was smart of her?"

The lady held out her hand and said, "I'm so glad to know you, dear."

I said, "I'm glad to know you, too."

Miss Stover patted her mother's hand and said to me, "Now we'll go and let Mom have a nap, and you'll help me in the kitchen."

I followed her to the kitchen. Miss Stover said, "Oh, Annie, here's a job for you. Spread peanut butter on this bread for me."

Just as if she was expecting me to come and help her make a party for the little kids. She said, "I know you have a lot to tell me, but I thought we'd wait until later when we can sit down and talk quietly. But one thing I would like to know, is your grandmother all right?"

I said yes, Grandma was fine. Then she said, "And does she know you are here?"

I shook my head no, and suddenly I felt terribly ashamed. What a thing to do, to come all the way out here without telling Grandma! Of course it was still early and she thought we were at the movies, but what would she think when we didn't get home? She'd be scared to death! I hadn't thought of that.

"Oh, Miss Stover, I said we were going to the show. I have to let her know. We'll be late getting home and she'll be wondering where we are.''

Miss Stover nodded and said, ''Yes, she'll be upset. I know you were upset, or you would have told her, but it isn't too late. We can call her up. It's only three o'clock, so we have time. Now put those sandwiches on a plate, and we'll put out some cookies and milk and take them all out to the yard.''

We carried the things out and put them on a table they had in the yard, and called all the kids. They all came running. You'd think Stevie had lived there all his life. He was just as dirty as the rest of them and he came running, with Skipper jumping and barking after him.

"Come on, everybody," Miss Stover said. "Fall to."

They sat down and started cleaning up the sandwiches, and Miss Stover asked Stevie how he liked the train ride. He started telling them all about it, how we didn't have a timetable, but ran and caught the train, and how the conductor swung his arm to tell the engineer to go, and how he stood in the doorway and shouted the station stops. That kid didn't miss a thing.

Miss Stover told them, "You know, Stevie lives

right near the railroad. He can go up on the roof and see the trains go by. Don't they look nice all lit up at night, Stevie?"

He said, with his mouth full of bread, "I'm gonna be a train man when I grow up. And anybody that throws rocks at the trains — I'm gonna put them in jail!"

"That's right, Stevie!" said Miss Stover.

This is only part of the book, **My Brother Stevie,** *by Eleanor Clymer. You can find out more about Annie, Stevie, and Miss Stover by reading the whole book.*

AUTHOR

Eleanor Clymer was born in New York City and has lived in cities most of her life. She now lives in the country and likes it, but she is still fond of city life, too. She feels that city children and country children are alike in many ways and that they share the same needs and feelings.

Mrs. Clymer always enjoyed writing from the time she worked for her high-school newspaper. She has written more than thirty-five books for children. Some of them are *The Big Pile of Dirt; Belinda's New Spring Hat; Chipmunk in the Forest; Me and the Eggman; Spider, The Cave, and the Pottery Bowl;* and *Wheels: A Book to Begin On.*

The Lion

There was a lion . . .
What kind of lion?
Very ferocious,
Grim and atrocious.
How terrible, how terrible!

Don't ask what he ate —
If he liked it . . . too late!
A tram and a track,
A cloud for a snack.
How terrible, how terrible!

He stepped with three legs,
He watched with three eyes,
He listened with three ears.
How terrible, how terrible!

Sharp teeth, evil eye,
He'd pass nothing by.
How terrible, how terrible!

Brana one day
Rubbed him away
With his eraser.
How terrible, how terrible!

– Dusan Radovic

a poem by a child from Yugoslavia

Inspector Peckit
by Don Freeman

High atop a chimney stack, a bright-eyed pigeon named Peckit stood gazing out over the rooftops of Paris, cooing to himself in French.

Being a clever detective, Peckit was forever seeking new mysteries to solve. Even at this moment he was observing a sad little girl with tears in her eyes, who was looking out of a window nearby.

Peckit sensed instantly that something was wrong. Always eager to be of help, he flew over and alighted on the window ledge.

"Peckit's the name," he said politely. "Inspector Peckit at your beck and call. Why, may I ask, are you crying?"

"Oh, you wouldn't understand," replied the girl. "I lost my new knit bag today, and I can't find it anywhere. It was a birthday gift from my grandmother."

Cocking his head to one side and speaking in both impeccable French and in pigeon English, Peckit corrected her. "*Pardonnez-moi, mademoiselle,* I'm a Private Eye detective, and finding lost articles is part of my job. Now, tell me, what is your name and where do you think you lost your bag? And what does it look like?"

"My name is Annette," the girl answered, wiping away her tears. "I think I must have lost my bag in the Luxembourg Gardens where I play. Or maybe I dropped it on the way home. It's small and round and white."

While Peckit was making a mental note of these clues, he noticed a fluffy cat curled up on the floor. "Confidentially, *mademoiselle,*" he said, "I must tell you that I already suspect your cat. When it comes to small round things, cats are not to be trusted."

Annette was horrified. "Oh, no, Inspector! Cattiva would never hide anything from me. *Jamais! Jamais!* Never!"

Peckit eyed the cat sternly.

"Have no fear, my friend," he said, spreading his wings. "This mystery will be solved before the day's end."

Peckit flew straight to the Luxembourg Gardens and landed on a bench. He peered suspiciously at everyone around him, which is the way detectives are likely to behave. Not far away a squirrel picked up a small, round object and quickly stowed it inside a hole in a tree.

"Aha!" said Peckit. "There's the scoundrel!"

But when he peeked into the hole to inspect, something nipped him hard on the beak!

"Oh, *excusez-moi!*" he squeaked. "I've made a mistake!"

Although his feathers were ruffled, Peckit was undaunted.

Suddenly, right there on the ground below him, he spied a small, round, white thing. Down he swooped and snatched up a ball of string that a boy was about to tie onto a toy sailboat.

Then Peckit flew directly to Annette's window.

"*Voilà!*" he said as he set the ball of string upon the windowsill. "Here is your lost bag. It was nothing at all. Call on Peckit any time!" He strutted along the sill with his tail feathers spread out like a proud peacock.

"Oh, no, Inspector! I'm sorry, but this isn't my knit bag," said Annette. "My bag is made of yarn, not string." And she showed him a soft ball of yarn.

Needless to say, Peckit was embarrassed. Especially with that cat Cattiva watching him!

Before taking flight, he poked his head inside the window and gave her his most suspecting look.

Peckit returned the ball of string to the surprised boy with the sailboat and then flew off to a safe perch above a cafe.

To his amazement, right below him on a

table, he saw something round and white and yarnlike!

With the swiftness of a gust of wind, Peckit swept down and picked up what he was sure was Annette's lost bag . . . .

It was spaghetti heaped high on a dish!

Of course, Peckit immediately realized his mistake. Never had he tasted anything so delicious!

After finishing the last strand of spaghetti, he set out once again to solve the mystery of the missing knit bag.

The shadows of the day were lengthening now, making it difficult for even a sharp-eyed detective to see clearly. Nevertheless, Peckit went snooping along the streets from doorway to doorway.

All at once he stopped in his tracks. There, at the entrance to a bakery, he spotted something soft and round and yarnlike. This time he was absolutely certain it was the lost bag. And just as he was about to snatch it . . . up it hopped and trotted away!

"Fooled again!" snapped Peckit disgustedly. "And by a fancy French poodle!"

It was almost dark now, and before continuing his search, Peckit decided to check in with his mate Viv. He knew she would be waiting for him on their perch in the Eiffel Tower. Spreading his wings wide, he floated down to a perfect landing.

There on the scaffolding was Viv, cozily resting inside a nest he had never seen before.

"Where in the world did you ever find such an elegant nest, my dove?" Peckit asked.

"It's lovely, *n'est-ce pas?*" she cooed. "I found it under a bench in the park this morning."

"In the park?" screeched Peckit, his eyes lighting up like flaming pinwheels. "That isn't a nest! It's the soft, round, white knit bag I've been searching for all day. It belongs to Annette, and I must get it back to her right away."

Viv knew better than to question a working detective. She quickly hopped aside and watched as Peckit flew across the moonlit sky, carrying the rumpled bag in his beak.

He landed with a flutter on Annette's windowsill, but all was dark and still inside the room. Setting down the bag, he gently pecked on the windowpane.

"Is that you, Inspector Peckit?" called Annette.

She jumped out of bed and ran to open the window wide.

"You found it! You found my birthday bag!" she exclaimed with joy. "Oh, *merci beaucoup!* Wherever did you find it?"

"Ah, *ma cherie*, we won't go into that!" chirped Peckit modestly. "Let's just say it was all in a day's work."

For a minute Annette couldn't think how best to thank her friend. "Here, *mon ami*," she said finally, holding up a ball of soft blue yarn. "Maybe you can use this to build a nest some-day."

Cattiva was awake now, too. "I wish your cat would stop looking at me so suspiciously," he said. "She acts as if I stole the knit bag."

"Oh, don't mind Cattiva," Annette said kindly. "That's just her natural look."

Peckit felt much better. He preened his feathers and bid Annette *bon soir*. He even gave Cattiva a parting wink before he flew back across the sleeping city of Paris to where Viv was waiting patiently.

"Oh Pecky!" she cooed when she saw the gift he had brought her. "Now we will have the coziest nest in the Eiffel Tower!"

Don Freeman has always been interested in the theatre. At one time he earned money in New York by drawing pictures of actors in scenes from Broadway plays. One reason he enjoys writing and illustrating books for children is that he can make up scenes and characters just the way he wants them. "I can create my own theatre in picture books," he says.

Mr. Freeman was first a musician in a jazz band. While he was going to art school during the day, he earned money by playing his trumpet at night. He had been trying to decide whether he should become an artist or a musician. One day he was drawing a picture as he rode on a New York subway. He was so interested in what he was doing that he forgot about everything else. After he had gotten off at his stop, he realized that he had left his trumpet on the subway. He never got it back. He says, "It was then that I decided to make my living as an artist!"

Don Freeman has written and illustrated many books. *Fly High, Fly Low*, also about city pigeons, was a Caldecott runner-up. Some of his other books are *Hattie the Backstage Bat, Mop Top, Norman the Doorman*, and *Penguins of All People*. Don Freeman and his wife Lydia live in California and have one son. Lydia Freeman is also a writer, and together the Freemans wrote *Pet of the Met*. They say that they often get story ideas from experiences in their own family. Mr. Freeman wrote *Inspector Peckit* soon after a visit to France.

BOOKS TO ENJOY

SEA FULL OF WHALES *by Richard Armour*

These poems are full of fun, but they also speak out about the need to preserve the many kinds of whales.

TAMMY CAMPS IN THE ROCKY MOUNTAINS
by Elizabeth Baker

Camping in the Rockies is fun, and even a little danger-ous, as Tammy photographs a bear face to face.

THE CASE OF THE ELEVATOR DUCK
by Polly Berrien Berends

A young detective tracks down the owner of a lost duck in a housing project where no pets are allowed.

HARLEQUIN AND THE GIFT OF MANY COLORS
by Remy Charlip and Burton Supree

This story tells how Harlequin, a poor boy who has no costume to wear at the carnival, appears in the most colorful patchwork suit ever seen.

THE CARP IN THE BATHTUB *by Barbara Cohen*

Could you eat the fish you kept alive in the bathtub till Passover? Leah and Harry have this problem, and it's both funny and sad.

THE WUMP WORLD *by Bill Peet*

The Wump creatures and their lovely Wump world are invaded by Pollutians from the planet Pollutus.

HIGGLETY PIGGLETY POP! *by Maurice Sendak*

A dog named Jennie, bored with her life, runs away and becomes a star in the Mother Goose Theatre.

Cavalcade

Cavalcade

Petronella

by Jay Williams

In the kingdom of Skyclear Mountain, three princes were always born to the king and queen. The oldest prince was always called Michael, the middle prince was always called George, and the youngest was always called Peter. When they were grown, they always went out to seek their fortunes. What happened to the oldest prince and the middle prince no one ever knew. But the youngest prince always rescued a princess, brought her home, and in time ruled over the kingdom. That was the way it had always been. And so far as anyone knew, that was the way it would always be.

Until now.

Now was the time of King Peter the twenty-sixth and Queen Blossom. An oldest prince was born, and a middle prince. But the youngest prince turned out to be a girl.

"Well," said the king gloomily, "we can't call her Peter. We'll have to call her Petronella. And what's to be done about it, I'm sure I don't know."

There was nothing to be done. The years passed, and the time came for the princes to go out and seek their fortunes. Michael and

George said good-by to the king and queen and mounted their horses. Then out came Petronella. She was dressed in traveling clothes, with her bag packed and a sword by her side.

"If you think," she said, "that I'm going to sit at home, you are mistaken. I'm going to seek my fortune, too."

"Impossible!" said the king.

"What will people say?" cried the queen.

"Look," said Prince Michael. "Be reasonable, Pet. Stay home. Sooner or later a prince will turn up here."

Petronella smiled. She was a tall, handsome girl with flaming red hair, and when she smiled in that particular way it meant she was trying to keep her temper.

"I'm going with you," she said. "I'll find a prince if I have to rescue one from something myself. And that's that."

The grooms brought out her horse. She said

good-by to her parents, and away she went behind her two brothers.

They traveled into the flatlands below Skyclear Mountain. After many days, they entered a great dark forest. They came to a place where the road divided into three, and there at the fork sat a little, wrinkled old man covered with dust and spiderwebs.

"Where do these roads go, old man?" inquired Prince Michael.

"The road on the right goes to the city of Gratz," the man replied. "The road in the center goes to the castle of Blitz. The road on the left goes to the house of Albion the enchanter. And that's one."

"What do you mean by 'And that's one'?" asked Prince George.

"I mean," said the old man, "that I am forced to sit on this spot without stirring, and that I must answer one question from each person who passes by. And that's two."

Petronella's kind heart was touched. "Is there anything I can do to help you?" she asked.

The old man sprang to his feet. The dust fell from him in clouds.

"You have already done so," he said. "For that question is the one which releases me. I have sat here for sixty-two years waiting for someone to ask me that." He snapped his fingers with joy. "In return, I will tell you anything you wish to know."

"Where can I find a prince?" Petronella said promptly.

"There is one in the house of Albion the enchanter," the old man answered.

"Ah," said Petronella, "then that is where I am going."

"In that case I will leave you," said her oldest brother. "For I am going to the castle of Blitz to see if I can find my fortune there."

"Good luck," said Prince George. "For I am going to the city of Gratz. I have a feeling my fortune is there,"

They embraced her and rode away.

Petronella looked thoughtfully at the old man, who was combing spiderwebs and dust out of his beard. "May I ask you something else?" she said.

"Of course. Anything."

"Suppose I wanted to rescue that prince from the enchanter. How would I go about it? I haven't any experience in such things, you see."

The old man chewed a piece of his beard. "I do not know everything," he said, after a moment. "I know that there are three magical secrets which, if you get them from him, will help you."

"How can I get them?" asked Petronella.

"Offer to work for him. He will set you three tasks, and if you can do them you may demand a reward for each. You must ask him for a comb for your hair, a mirror to look into, and a ring for your finger."

"And then?"

"I do not know. I only know that when you rescue the prince, you can use these things to escape from the enchanter."

"It doesn't sound easy," sighed Petronella.

"Nothing we really want is easy," said the old man. "Look at me — I have wanted my freedom, and I've had to wait sixty-two years for it."

Petronella said good-bye to him. She mounted her horse and galloped along the third road.

It ended at a large house with a red roof. It was a comfortable-looking house, surrounded by gardens and stables and trees heavy with fruit.

On the lawn sat a very handsome young man with his eyes closed and his face turned to the sky.

Petronella tied her horse to the gate and walked across the lawn.

"Is this the house of Albion the enchanter?" she said.

The young man blinked up at her in surprise.

"I think so," he said. "Yes, I'm sure it is."

"And who are you?"

The young man yawned and stretched. "I am Prince Ferdinand of Firebright," he replied. "Would you mind stepping aside? I'm trying to get a suntan and you're standing in the way."

Petronella snorted. "You don't sound like much of a prince," she said.

"That's funny," said the young man, closing his eyes. "That's what my father always says."

At that moment the door of the house opened. Out came a man dressed all in black and silver. He was tall and thin, and as sinister as a cloud full of thunder. His face was stern, but full of

wisdom. Petronella knew at once that he must be the enchanter.

He bowed to her politely. "What can I do for you?"

"I wish to work for you," said Petronella boldly.

Albion nodded. "I cannot refuse you," he said. "But I warn you, it will be dangerous. Tonight I will give you a task. If you do it, I will reward you. If you fail, you must die."

Petronella glanced at the prince and sighed. "If I must, I must," she said. "Very well."

That evening they all had dinner together in the enchanter's cozy kitchen. Then Albion took Petronella out to a stone building and unbolted its door. Inside were seven huge black dogs.

"You must watch my hounds all night," said he.

Petronella went in, and Albion closed and locked the door.

At once the hounds began to snarl and bark. They showed their teeth at her. But Petronella was a real princess. She plucked up her courage. Instead of backing away, she went toward the dogs. She began to speak to them in a quiet voice. They stopped snarling and sniffed at her. She patted their heads.

"I see what it is," she said. "You are lonely here. I will keep you company."

And so all night long, she sat on the floor and talked to the hounds and stroked them. They lay close to her, panting.

In the morning Albion came and let her out. "Ah," said he, "I see that you are brave. If you had run from the dogs, they would have torn you to pieces. Now you may ask for what you want."

"I want a comb for my hair," said Petronella.

The enchanter gave her a comb carved from a piece of black wood.

Prince Ferdinand was sunning himself and working at a crossword puzzle. Petronella said to him in a low voice, "I am doing this for you."

"That's nice," said the prince. "What's 'selfish' in nine letters?"

"You are," snapped Petronella. She went to the enchanter. "I will work for you once more," she said.

That night Albion led her to a stable. Inside were seven huge horses.

"Tonight," he said, "you must watch my horses."

He went out and locked the door. At once the horses began to rear and neigh. They pawed at her with their iron hoofs.

But Petronella was a real princess. She looked closely at them and saw that their coats were rough and their manes and tails full of burrs.

"I see what it is," she said. "You are hungry and dirty."

She brought them as much hay as they could eat, and began to brush them. All night long she fed them and groomed them, and they stood quietly in their stalls.

In the morning Albion let her out. He looked at her with admiration. "You are as kind as you are brave," said he. "If you had run from them, they would have trampled you under their hoofs. What will you have as a reward?"

"I want a mirror to look into," said Petronella.

The enchanter gave her a mirror made of gray silver.

She looked across the lawn at Prince Ferdinand. He was doing setting-up exercises. He was certainly handsome. She said to the enchanter, "I will work for you once more."

That night Albion led her to a loft above the stables. There, on perches, were seven great hawks.

"Tonight," said he, "you must watch my hawks."

As soon as Petronella was locked in, the hawks began to beat their wings and scream at her.

Petronella laughed. "That is not how birds sing," she said. "Listen."

She began to sing in a sweet voice. The hawks fell silent. All night long she sang to them, and they sat like feathered statues on their perches, listening.

In the morning Albion said, "You are as talented as you are kind and brave. If you had run from them, they would have pecked and clawed you without mercy. What do you want now?"

"I want a ring for my finger," said Petronella.

The enchanter gave her a ring made from a single diamond.

All that day and all that night Petronella

slept, for she was very tired. But early the next morning, she crept into Prince Ferdinand's room. He was sound asleep, wearing purple pajamas.

"Wake up," whispered Petronella. "I am going to rescue you."

Ferdinand awoke and stared sleepily at her. "What time is it?"

"Never mind that. Come on!" she said.

"But I'm sleepy," Ferdinand objected. "And it's so pleasant here."

Petronella shook her head. "You're not much of a prince," she said grimly. "But you're the best I can do."

She grabbed him by the arm and dragged him out of bed and down the stairs. His horse and hers were in a separate stable, and she saddled them quickly. She gave the prince a shove, and he mounted. She jumped on her own horse, grabbed the prince's reins, and away they went like the wind.

They had not gone far when they heard a tremendous thumping. Petronella looked back. A dark cloud rose behind them, and beneath it she saw the enchanter. He was running with great strides, faster than the horses could go.

Petronella desperately pulled out her comb. "The old man said this would help me!" she said. And because she didn't know what else to do with it, she threw the comb on the ground.

Immediately a forest rose up. The trees were so thick that no one could get between them.

Away went Petronella and the prince. But the enchanter turned himself into an ax and began to chop. Right and left he chopped, flashing, and the trees fell before him.

Soon he was through the wood, and once again Petronella heard his footsteps thumping behind.

She reined in the horses. She took out the mirror and threw it on the ground. At once a wide lake spread out behind them, gray and shining.

Off they went again. But the enchanter sprang into the water, turning himself into a fish as he did so. He swam across the lake and leaped out of the water on the other bank. Petronella heard him coming — *thump! thump!* — behind them again.

This time she threw down the ring. It didn't turn into anything, but lay shining on the ground.

The enchanter came running up. As he jumped over the ring, it opened wide and then snapped up around him. It held his arms tight to his body, in a magical grip from which he could not escape.

"Well," said Prince Ferdinand, "that's the end of him."

Petronella looked at him in annoyance. Then she looked at the enchanter, held fast in the ring.

"Bother!" she said. "I can't just leave him here. He'll starve to death."

She got off her horse and went up to him.

"If I release you," she said, "will you promise to let the prince go free?"

Albion stared at her in astonishment. "Let him go free?" he said. "What are you talking about? I'm glad to get rid of him."

It was Petronella's turn to look surprised. "I don't understand," she said. "Weren't you holding him prisoner?"

"Certainly not," said Albion. "He came to visit me for a weekend. At the end of it, he said, 'It's so pleasant here, do you mind if I stay on for another day or two?' I'm very polite and I said, 'Of course.' He stayed on, and on, and on. I didn't like to be rude to a guest and I couldn't just kick him out. I don't know what I'd have done if you hadn't dragged him away."

"But then — " said Petronella, "but then — why did you come running after him this way?"

"I wasn't chasing *him*," said the enchanter. "I was chasing *you*. You are just the girl I've been looking for. You are brave and kind and talented, and beautiful as well."

"Oh," said Petronella.

"I see," she said.

"Hmm," she said. "How do I get this ring off you?"

"Give me a kiss," said the enchanter.

She did so. The ring vanished from around Albion and reappeared on Petronella's finger.

"I don't know what my parents will say when I come home with you instead of a prince," she said.

"Let's go and find out, shall we?" said the enchanter cheerfully.

He mounted one horse and Petronella the other. And off they trotted, side by side, leaving Prince Ferdinand of Firebright to walk home as best he could.

Jay Williams was born in Buffalo, New York, and now has a home in Connecticut. He and his wife also live part of the time in a cottage in England. Besides writing, Mr. Williams enjoys building model ships and collecting Japanese and Chinese paintings. He is also president of a field archery club in Connecticut.

When he was young, Mr. Williams was in vaudeville. Vaudeville was a kind of stage show that was very popular about forty or fifty years ago. A vaudeville show had many different performers such as singers, dancers, and jugglers. Mr. Williams was a comedian. That may be one reason why he enjoys writing books that make people laugh.

During World War II, Mr. Williams was in the U. S. Infantry and was wounded in Germany. By this time, he had begun to make his living by writing full-time. He has written many books for both adults and children. Some of his books that you will enjoy are *The Silver Whistle, Stupid Marco, The Practical Princess,* and *The King with Six Friends.* In addition, he and another writer, Raymond Abrashkin, created the popular Danny Dunn series. *Danny Dunn and the Fossil Cave* and *Danny Dunn on the Ocean Floor* are both winners of the Young Readers' Choice Awards from the Pacific Northwest Library Association. One of his books for older boys and girls, *The Hawkstone,* received the Lewis Carroll Shelf Award.

Skill
Lesson:

MAKING MENTAL PICTURES

In at least one way, a person who writes a story is like an artist who paints pictures. Each of them tries to make pictures for us. An artist uses paints to make real pictures. A person who writes a story uses words to help us make pictures in our minds.

There are real pictures in almost any story you will read. But those pictures do not show everything that the words tell about. To understand and enjoy a story as much as you can, you will need to imagine what things in the story would look like if you really saw them. Doing this can be called **making mental pictures.**

The words in a story will tell you much that you can use to help you make such mental pictures. Any picture you imagine of a person, thing, or happening in a story should fit well with what the words say. It should not have in it anything that does not agree with those words.

As you read the following paragraph, imagine a picture of the cowboy who is being talked about:

The first real cowboy Billy ever saw didn't look the way he thought a cowboy would look. He was tall, but he was standing beside a jeep instead of sitting on a horse. He was wearing blue pants that looked like those Billy wore to school. He had on a red shirt that was open at the neck. He wasn't wearing a hat, and he didn't have guns or a rope. Billy was glad to see, though, that he was wearing brown cowboy boots. That made him seem more like a cowboy.

Could you make a picture in your mind of the cowboy that Billy saw?

Here are pictures of four cowboys. Which picture is most like the one you made in your mind?

Discussion

Help your class answer these questions:

1. How are an artist and a person who writes a story alike?

2. How can making pictures in your mind help you as you read a story?

3. What should be true about pictures you imagine as you read a story?

4. What can you do to help you imagine pictures that are good ones?

5. Which picture shows the cowboy that Billy saw? How did you know that each of the others was wrong?

On your own

As you read the following, imagine pictures that would fit the things that are happening.

Bob was trying to fix the chain on his new red bicycle. He had it turned upside down on the grass as he worked. A big brown dog walked up to him and said, "You'll have to take the back wheel off before you can fix the chain."

Bob was so surprised that he didn't know what to do. Just then the man who owned the dog came up. When Bob told him what the dog had said, the man said, "Don't listen to him. He doesn't know how to fix a bicycle."

Checking your work

Which of the following rows of pictures is most like the pictures that you made in your mind? Tell your class why you picked the pictures that you did.

The Case of the Mysterious Tramp

by Donald J. Sobol

His head bent low over the handlebars of his bike, Encyclopedia Brown rounded the corner of Beech Street like high-speed sandpaper.

It was three minutes before six o'clock of a summer evening. With a bit of luck and a following wind, Encyclopedia hoped to make it home on time for dinner.

Suddenly someone called his name.

"Leroy! Leroy Brown!"

Right off he knew it had to be a teacher calling. Only teachers and his mother and father called him Leroy.

Everyone else in the town of Idaville called him Encyclopedia.

He didn't look much like an encyclopedia, which is a set of books filled with all kinds of facts. People called him Encyclopedia because he had read more books than a bathtubful of professors. And he never forgot anything he read.

"Leroy! Leroy!"

It was Mrs. Worth, his old second-grade teacher. She was standing beside her car, looking very sad.

"I can't get it going," she said. "Can you help me?"

"I'll try," said Encyclopedia. He leaned his bike against a tree and raised the hood of the car.

"Start her again, please, Mrs. Worth," he said. The motor coughed and sputtered out.

"The trouble must be in the carburetor," said Encyclopedia, beginning to disappear under the hood.

He lifted off the air filter. Now he could reach the butterfly valve in the carburetor. He poked it open with his finger.

The motor roared to life when Mrs. Worth again tried to start it.

Mrs. Worth was delighted. When Encyclopedia returned to view, she thanked him over and over again.

"Oh, it wasn't anything," said Encyclopedia. "Just a stuck valve."

He smiled as Mrs. Worth drove off — till he looked at his watch. It gave him unsmiling news. It was past six o'clock, the Browns' dinner hour. He'd catch it for being late!

His mother put down a pot of boiled cabbage to stare at him. Dirt and grease from Mrs. Worth's motor coated him from ears to sneakers.

"Where have you been?" she asked, kissing the one clean spot on his cheek.

"Riding my bike," answered Encyclopedia.

He didn't mention Mrs. Worth's motor. He hardly ever spoke to anyone, not even his parents, about the help he gave others. And he *never* spoke about the help he gave grown-ups.

His mother looked out at Rover Avenue through the kitchen window. Strangely enough, she hadn't scolded him for being late.

"Your father knows we are having corned beef and cabbage tonight," she said in a worried voice. "What could be keeping him?"

"Dad wouldn't miss his favorite dish without a good reason," said Encyclopedia. "Maybe he's chasing a dangerous crook or something."

Mrs. Brown looked even more worried.

Encyclopedia tried again. "Don't worry, Mom," he said. "Dad is the best police officer in the state. He'll be home soon."

Encyclopedia was right. As he was washing the back of his neck, he heard his father close the garage door.

A moment later, Mr. Brown entered the house. He was a big, broad-shouldered man dressed in a police chief's uniform.

His uniform was the envy of every law officer in the United States. Although Idaville was like many other American towns, its police force was *unlike* any other.

For more than a year, neither child nor grown-up had gotten away with breaking a law.

Hardened criminals had passed the word: "Stay clear of Idaville."

This was partly because the Idaville police officers were well trained, smart, and brave. But mostly it was because Chief Brown had Encyclopedia at the dinner table.

Chief Brown never whispered a word of how Encyclopedia helped him. After all, who would believe the truth?

Who would believe that a young boy solved difficult cases while eating dinner in the Browns' red brick house on Rover Avenue?

Naturally, Encyclopedia never let out that he was the mastermind behind Idaville's war on crime. So the name Leroy Brown was missing from the honor roll of the world's great detectives.

"I'm sorry to be late, dear," said Chief Brown as he sat down to eat. "A terrible thing happened this afternoon. Mr. Clancy, the plumber, was beaten and robbed."

"Was he badly hurt?" asked Mrs. Brown.

"He's in the city hospital," Chief Brown said. "The doctors say he'll be all right. I'm afraid we'll never catch the man who attacked him."

"Why not, Dad?" asked Encyclopedia. "Didn't anyone see what happened?"

"John Morgan saw everything," said Chief Brown.

"He's Mr. Clancy's helper. He was sitting in the truck when a tramp attacked Mr. Clancy."

Chief Brown unbuttoned his breast pocket and drew out his notebook. "I wrote down everything John Morgan told me. I'll read it to you."

Encyclopedia closed his eyes. He always closed his eyes when he did his heavy thinking on a case.

His father began to read what John Morgan had told him about the beating and theft:

"Clancy was driving the truck, and I was sitting beside him. We had turned onto the dirt road near the Benson farm when the motor overheated. Clancy stopped, walked around to the front of the truck, and lifted the hood. As he took off the radiator cap, a tramp jumped out of the woods. The tramp struck Clancy on the head with a piece of pipe.

"Clancy fell over the radiator and slid down the front of the truck. I leaped out of the truck, but the tramp was already racing into the woods. He carried the pipe and Clancy's billfold. I let him go in order to get Clancy to the hospital right away."

Chief Brown finished reading and closed his notebook.

Encyclopedia opened his eyes. He asked but one question: "Did Mr. Clancy have an unusually large amount of money in his billfold?"

His father looked startled.

"Why, yes," he answered. "It so happened that Mr. Clancy had two hundred dollars in his billfold. He had just been paid for work on a new apartment house. What made you think he was carrying a lot of money?"

"He had to be," said Encyclopedia. "Now you should have no trouble finding the man who struck and robbed him."

"No trouble?" said Chief Brown. "The woods come out on the railroad tracks. It's a sure bet that the tramp hopped a ride on a freight train. He's probably in another state by now."

"You'll find him where John Morgan lives — and the two hundred dollars besides," said Encyclopedia.

"Do you think John Morgan helped the tramp rob Mr. Clancy?" asked Mrs. Brown.

"No," answered Encyclopedia.

"Well, what do you think?" asked Chief Brown.

"I think that when Mr. Clancy stopped the truck in the woods, John Morgan saw his chance," answered Encyclopedia. "While Mr. Clancy was checking the radiator, John Morgan sneaked from the truck, knocked him out, and stole his billfold with the two hundred dollars."

"What about the tramp?" asked Chief Brown.

"There never was a tramp, Dad," said Encyclopedia. "John Morgan made him up. John Morgan robbed Mr. Clancy by himself and then drove him to the hospital."

Chief Brown rubbed his chin thoughtfully. "That could be what really happened," he said. "But I can't prove it."

"The proof is down in black and white," said Encyclopedia. "Just read over what John Morgan told you. He gives himself away!"

HOW DID JOHN MORGAN GIVE HIMSELF AWAY?

(Turn the page for the solution to "The Case of the Mysterious Tramp.")

AUTHOR

Born in New York City, Donald J. Sobol first worked for a newspaper and then for a department store. He then decided to become a writer. He has been glad of it ever since, because his books have been very popular. He also writes stories and articles for newspapers and magazines.

Mr. Sobol and his wife and four children live in Florida. The Sobols own two cars — both made in the year 1930! Old cars are not only Mr. Sobol's hobby, but they are put to good use. He drives one of them every weekday, and he says that the other one is his "Sunday car."

The story you just read from is from *Encyclopedia Brown Finds the Clues.* Other books about this young hero are:

Encyclopedia Brown: Boy Detective

Encyclopedia Brown Shows the Way

Encyclopedia Brown Takes the Case

Encyclopedia Brown Tracks Them Down

Encyclopedia Brown Solves Them All

Solution to "The Case of the Mysterious Tramp"

John Morgan said that Mr. Clancy walked around to the front of the truck and raised the hood.

He described how "Clancy fell over the radiator and slid down the front of the truck" after being struck by the tramp. Then he himself "climbed out of the truck."

But he said he had been sitting in the front seat. So he saw the attack through the windshield.

Impossible!

The hood of the truck was raised, remember?

All John Morgan could have seen through the windshield was the hood!

Chief Brown recovered Mr. Clancy's money. The guilty John Morgan was sent to jail.

Brother

I had a little brother
And I brought him to my mother
And I said I want another
Little brother for a change.
But she said don't be a bother
So I took him to my father
And I said this little bother
Of a brother's very strange.
But he said one little brother
Is exactly like another
And every little brother
Misbehaves a bit he said.
So I took the little bother
From my mother and my father
And I put the little bother
Of a brother back to bed.

– *Mary Ann Hoberman*

263

SOME OLD

1. I've taken trips to China,
To England and Nepal.
I've been to every country
Although I'm very small.
Others pay my travel fees —
I thank you one and all!
   What am I?

2. Seven pears hanging high;
Seven men came riding by.
Each took a pear, and left six hanging there.
   How do you explain this?

RIDDLES

3. As I was going to St. Ives
   I met a man with seven wives.
   Every wife had seven sacks;
   Every sack had seven cats;
   Every cat had seven kits.
   Kits — cats — sacks — and wives —
   How many were going to St. Ives?

1. A postage stamp.
2. "Each" was the name of one of the men.
3. One: the narrator of the poem. The poem never says that anyone else was going to St. Ives.

A folktale from India

Old Mother Parvati (Par-vah'tee) was a Bhilla (bee'lah). The Bhillas are a tribe of brown-skinned, dark-eyed people who live on the edge of the jungle in central India. Old Mother Parvati lived all alone in a mud-walled, thatch-roofed hut in the shadow of the dark, animal-filled jungle. But she was not afraid, because she had lived a long time and was very wise,

266

and because she had the gift of magic. For Mother Parvati possessed a magic wand and a magic pumpkin.

The magic wand looked just like any other magic wand, but the magic pumpkin was something to behold! It had a door which really opened, and windows you could see through, and it was so large that Mother Parvati could ride comfortably inside. Whenever she wanted to go somewhere, she would open the door of

the magic pumpkin, step inside, and say, *"Chal ra, Bhopalla, tunuk, tunuk!"* (Chal-rah', Boh-pah'la, too-nook', too-nook'). This means, "Come on, Pumpkin, turn faster, turn faster!" And then the magic pumpkin would begin to roll along the ground, faster and faster. When it stopped, Mother Parvati would find herself wherever she wanted to be.

One day Mother Parvati decided to visit her married daughter in the village of Ghar-Bengal (gar ben-gawl'). Ghar-Bengal was quite a long distance away from Mother Parvati's hut, unless you traveled straight through the jungle, which was very, very dangerous. But Mother Parvati had a great deal of confidence in her own wits and in her magic, so she decided to travel through the jungle anyway.

She arranged her hair in three long braids and wrapped a clean sari around her wiry brown body. She bundled a little pot of ghee into some jungle leaves as a gift for her daughter. Then she walked carefully through the cucumbers and eggplants and onions in her garden until she came to the enormous orange pumpkin. She opened the door and stepped inside.

"*Chal ra, Bhopalla, tunuk, tunuk!*" Mother Parvati said, and the pumpkin quavered and shook until the ground rumbled. Then the big orange pumpkin began to roll, at first slowly and then faster and faster, until the pumpkin and Mother Parvati inside were rolling along at a merry pace through the dark, mysterious jungle.

The rolling pumpkin made a loud whirring noise, and swarms of monkeys fled screaming

through the treetops overhead. Worried flocks of birds flew straight up into the clouds, and small animals tried to make themselves invisible under the jungle leaves. But there was one great beast who wasn't frightened by the noise, and that was Vagha (vah'ga), the great golden tiger. Curious, he padded toward the sound. When he saw the strange whirling pumpkin, he stopped it easily by placing his heavy golden paw on the pumpkin's lid.

When Mother Parvati saw a gleaming golden eye peering at her through one of the pumpkin's windows, she knew that Vagha, the Emperor of the jungle, had interrupted her journey. Calmly, the wise old lady waited for the tiger to speak, because she knew exactly what she was going to do.

"Aha!" the tiger roared. "All day long I've been puzzling over what I shall eat for dinner. And now my dinner sits before me — a nice, firm, brown, juicy old lady."

In a weak, quavery voice Mother Parvati replied, "Your eyes must be failing you, O Emperor of the jungle! I am a poor, scrawny, fleshless old woman who would hardly fill a

hole in your tooth." And with that Mother Parvati waved her magic wand just a little bit, and she did become fleshless and scrawny.

"Hmmmmm," said the tiger (but when the tiger said "hmmmmm" it sounded like a roar). "Now that I look a little closer, I see that you are not as juicy a meal as I first thought. But nevertheless I intend to eat you for my dinner."

"But Sir, why not wait a while?" Mother Parvati said. "I'm on my way to Ghar-Bengal to visit my married daughter, who is a marvelous cook. After a week or two at her house, I'll be round and plump, and a fitting meal for the Emperor of the jungle. Then, on my way back, you can eat me."

"Hmmmmm," said the tiger. "There's truth in what you say. But how do I know that you'll come back this way?"

"By the hair of Siva (see'va) I promise that I will return this way, in a week or two or three," she answered.

When the tiger heard Mother Parvati say that, he knew that he could trust her. As he lifted his heavy velvet paw from the top of the pumpkin, Mother Parvati whispered, *"Chal ra, Bhopalla, tunuk, tunuk!"* once again, and the journey through the jungle continued.

Once more the noisy whirring of the magic pumpkin upset the routine of the jungle. Crows cawed in astonishment. The flat, expressionless eyes of a cobra stared in disbelief. A leopard cub tripped over its own feet hurrying to get out of the way. But again there was one great beast who was not frightened, but only curious. Kolha (cole'a), the gray wolf, placed his large shaggy body in the path of the pumpkin and stopped it with a thud as it hit his side.

Mother Parvati was shaken a little by the sudden stop, but she had time to recognize the rough gray coat of the great wolf.

"Aha!" said the wolf (but his "aha" sounded like "ahoooowl"). "All this livelong day I have wondered what to have for my supper, and now my supper has arrived in an orange pumpkin. What good fortune!"

"But sir," Mother Parvati said in her weak, quavery voice. "My poor skinny old body could hardly satisfy the hunger of a huge, fierce beast like yourself." And once again she used her magic wand to make herself look fleshless and scrawny. "I am going to Ghar-Bengal to visit my daughter who cooks well enough to please a maharaja. After a few weeks with her I'll be plump and delicious. Why not wait until I return from my daughter's house, and eat me then?"

"But how can I be sure that you will return this way?" Kolha asked.

"By the beard of Vaghdeo (vog-day'oh) I promise to return!"

When he heard such a strong statement coming from the frail old lady, Kolha released her.

Soon the whirling pumpkin was on its way again, and in less time than it takes to tell, Mother Parvati had reached the hut of her daughter, Uma (oo′ma).

Mother and daughter lived in harmony for the next few weeks, and Mother Parvati *did* get plump eating Uma's good cooking. But when

it was time for Mother Parvati to return to her own home, Uma grew worried.

"Mother, I am so afraid the tiger and the wolf will be waiting to eat you," Uma said. "Please don't return through the jungle!"

But Mother Parvati only laughed. "I must return through the jungle, dear Uma. I have given my word." Seeing her daughter's troubled expression, she added, "Don't worry about me, my dear. I'm sure I am smarter than any beast in the jungle."

So into her pumpkin Mother Parvati stepped. Because she knew exactly how she would outwit the tiger and the wolf, she started the pumpkin with a *"Chal ra, Bhopalla, tunuk, tunuk,"* and then closed her eyes for a little nap.

Deep within the jungle Vagha, the tiger, had been waiting for Mother Parvati to arrive. His stomach was rumbling impatiently and his temper was very short. As he padded back and forth along the leafy path, he mumbled grumpily to himself.

"Ho there, Vagha," the gray wolf called. "Why are you pacing the jungle in such an angry mood?"

"Ho there yourself, Kolha," the tiger replied. "I'm waiting for an old lady in a pumpkin to come along."

"How very strange!" the wolf declared. "I'm waiting for an old lady in a pumpkin myself."

"This lady is going to be my dinner," said Vagha.

"How very strange indeed!" said Kolha. "This lady is going to be my supper."

"I don't sssssuppose it could be the sssssame old lady," the tiger hissed, showing his long, white teeth.

"I grrrreatly doubt it," the wolf growled, showing his sharp, pointed teeth.

"Then, Sirrrr, I shall eat the firrrrst old lady who appearrrrrs," purred the sly Vagha.

"You impudent spoil-sport!" sputtered Kolha. "You mustn't spoil the splendid supper I'm expecting!"

Just then the magic pumpkin whirled into view. Kolha and Vagha both pounced on it, bringing the pumpkin to a quick halt.

With an angry wolf staring through one window, and an angry tiger staring through the other, most people would have been terribly frightened. But Mother Parvati rubbed her eyes as though she had just awakened, and in a puzzled voice she asked, "Your Excellencies, what can I do for you?"

"You promised to be my dinner," Vagha snarled.

"You promised to be *my* supper," Kolha barked. "Now which one of us is going to eat you?"

Mother Parvati shook her head and blinked her eyes. She pretended to be very confused. "Oh dear! Oh dear me," she chirped. "I do remember promising one of you that you could eat me. But which one was it? When one gets to be my age, one's memory fails, you know."

"YOU PROMISED ME!" the tiger roared.

"I WAS THE ONE SHE PROMISED!" the gray wolf howled.

The huge beasts glared at one another, their noses only an inch apart. Kolha's fierce eyes blazed like the sun, and Vagha's fierce eyes glittered like glowing coals. The rough hair

along Vagha's spine rose straight up as Kolha slowly sank on his haunches preparing to leap. And then they sprang at one another. The stillness of the jungle was shattered with thuds, thumps, hisses, howls, screeches, shrieks, rattles, and roars as the animals spun in a mad round of clawing, scratching, biting, and tearing.

Mother Parvati watched the melee for a few moments, her dark eyes dancing with mischief.

Then she calmly said, *"Chal ra, Bhopalla, tunuk, tunuk."* With a rumble and a whir, the magic pumpkin rolled farther and farther away from the furious battle. At last the dark jungle was left behind, and the pumpkin rolled into the sunlit garden of wise Mother Parvati.

"Home at last!" she sighed contentedly as she stepped out of her magic pumpkin. "I never *did* intend to be anybody's dinner!"

AUTHOR

Gloria Skurzynski was born in Duquesne, Pennsylvania, and once worked for a steel company in Pittsburgh. She says that she began writing professionally after she became inspired by some poetry one of her daughters had written. Mrs. Skurzynski has written many articles and stories for magazines, and she is also the author of *The Remarkable Journey of Gustavus Bell. The Magic Pumpkin* is a well-known folktale from India that Mrs. Skurzynski has retold in her own interesting style of writing.

Gloria Skurzynski and her husband, who is an aerospace engineer, now live in Salt Lake City, Utah. They have five daughters: Serena, Janine, Joan, Alane, and Lauren.

THE WOODEN CAT MAN

by Sid Fleischman

This story is based on a true happening. The Chinese Year of the Water Ox was the same as the year 1913 on our calendar.

In the Year of the Water Ox, a long time ago, the sun was rising off the South China Sea. Roosters crowed like alarm clocks in a thousand villages.

The day of the Thing-in-the-Sky began.

Miss Singsong awoke. She listened for a moment. Grandfather was still snoring. He no longer heard the roosters as well as he used to.

"Wake up, Grandfather," she said at his ear. Then she tickled his nose with a sprig of orange blossoms. And finally he awoke.

"Good morning, child," he said. And then he added grumpily, "The roosters don't crow as loudly as they used to. When I was a boy, we had roosters with voices like trumpets. Like claps of thunder!"

"Yes, Grandfather."

He yawned and stretched and began to smile.

"Look there by the window, Miss Singsong," he said. It was his pet name for her. Wasn't she always humming or singing as she went about her chores? "I finished a new kite for you last night. Do you like it?"

Her dark eyes swept to the window. A great yellow butterfly rustled in the dawn breeze — a butterfly shaped of bamboo and silk.

Her heart gave a leap. "It's beautiful," she exclaimed. "Too beautiful to fly, Grandfather."

"It's only a kite," he laughed, and prepared himself for the day ahead.

Miss Singsong braided his long queue and fixed him a breakfast of bean curd and fresh honey and green tea. Then he set out with a string of rattraps thrown over his shoulder. In the villages scattered like nests among the fields and rice paddies he was known as The Wooden Cat Man.

Wooden cat was the Chinese name for rattrap.

"Buy my wooden cats!" he'd shout at farmhouses and shopkeepers and even outside the high walls of the Mandarin's home. "Catch your mice and rats with my fine wooden cats!"

As long as Miss Singsong could remember, Grandfather had peddled his rattraps from village to village. But that morning, as she ran with the new kite, it saddened her that Grandfather had grown old making and selling wooden cats.

The yellow butterfly lifted itself on the wind. Its wings fluttered as if it had come alive. She remembered kites Grandfather had made in the shapes of roaring dragons and golden fish with feathery tails.

And she thought — what an artist Grandfather was! If only he could spend all his days making the beautiful kites he loved instead of ugly rattraps.

Just then Miss Singsong stepped on a bee. For an instant she felt it buzz under her foot. Then, like a small shaft of lightning, it stung.

"Ai!" she cried out and hopped about on one foot. The butterfly kite dipped madly, and

quickly she tugged back on the string. Then, standing like a stork on one leg, she began winding the kite back to safety.

At the same time she became aware of an angry hum in the sky. The sound became louder and louder, crackling and popping like distant firecrackers. Villagers heard it, too, and ran out of doors. Farmers looked up from their work.

There was a thing in the sky!

At first Miss Singsong thought it was a great kite, flashing in the sun like a huge, silver moth. Quickly it drew closer, roaring over the villages, and everyone scurried like mice to hide.

But Miss Singsong, limping along, couldn't run fast enough. She was frightened and her heart beat wildly. The Thing was coming down as if to catch its own shadow racing along the field. A great wind swept over her, whipping her hair about. She clapped hands over her ears to shut out the terrible sound. Then she saw the Thing-in-the-Sky come to rest not far away.

The wind vanished. The noise stopped. The dust settled and she saw the tall figure of a man leap to the ground.

Her breath caught in a new flash of wonder and fear and surprise. If only she could run! If only she could hide! But she stood frozen to the spot, unable to move. She could only stare.

The man had eyes as round as teacups. He wore tall leather boots and a long leather coat. Even his head seemed to be made of polished leather.

He waved at her and shouted in a language that she had never heard before, "It's only a flying machine." He smiled, lifted his huge glass goggles, and pulled off his leather helmet. Hair tumbled out as pale as rice straw. "Haven't you ever seen an airplane before?"

She gazed at him in awe. She felt as rooted to the earth as a willow tree. Again a strange jumble of words tumbled from his lips.

"Do you want to go up for a ride?"

When the villagers saw that Miss Singsong did not run from the Thing-in-the-Sky, they came out of hiding. Even the Mandarin, in silk slippers and silk robe and silk cap, appeared with his attendants. He was a large and proud man, and approached the Thing-in-the-Sky with a great show of courage.

He bowed toward the man with goggles, and the man with the goggles bowed back. They spoke in their own languages, neither understanding the other.

"Welcome to our village," said the Mandarin.

Slowly the villagers began to crowd around, but no one dared to touch the Thing-in-the-Sky.

Except the Mandarin.

He ran his long, yellow fingernails over the wings and gazed into the cockpit. He clucked his tongue and nodded his head and pulled at his wispy beard.

The tall man said, "You see? There's nothing to be afraid of."

The Mandarin slipped his hands into his sleeves, and Miss Singsong heard him mutter, "It's a clever toy. Only a toy."

She could see envy in his eyes. Clearly he wished he owned such a clever toy.

The Mandarin feasted the tall man behind the walls and gardens of his great house. Villagers gathered around the moon gates. Rumors quickly spread from the servants that the Thing-in-the-Sky had come from Canton — in an hour. Not even an arrow could travel so fast!

Grandfather was returning to the village when the tall foreigner pulled on his leather helmet and glass goggles. He twirled the stick at the nose of his flying machine until it roared.

Miss Singsong hobbled up beside Grandfather. Together they stood in the wind as the clever toy sped along the field. It lifted its wheels off the earth and rose into the air. Moments later it disappeared with a long steady hum among the clouds.

"Grandfather!" Miss Singsong said suddenly. "The Mandarin says it is only a toy. But perhaps it was truly the *fung-hwang* come at last."

The *fung-hwang* was a fabled bird. No one in

all of China had ever seen one, except painted on ancient scrolls. For centuries people had waited for the *fung-hwang* to arrive, bringing with it good luck and good fortune.

"No," Grandfather snorted. "Isn't the *fung-hwang* a golden bird? And doesn't it have the tail of a peacock?" And then he added, "Why are you limping, child?"

"I stepped on a bee," she answered.

The Festival of Kites

That night, working in the light of a peanut-oil lamp, Grandfather attached springs to blocks of oak, creating wooden cats. In the morning he left with the string of rattraps thrown over his shoulder to go peddling among the villages.

It was almost noon when Miss Singsong heard a gong sounding from the Mandarin's great house. Like everyone else, she came running.

The Mandarin stood in the moon gate and addressed the villagers. "Will it not soon be the ninth day of the ninth moon? The Festival of Kites! I shall fly a kite like the one that visited here yesterday. Who is the best kite-maker among you, eh?"

All of the men and boys of the villages made kites to fly on the ninth day of the ninth moon.

Miss Singsong quickly stepped forward. "My grandfather!" she announced.

Almost everyone laughed. "The Wooden Cat Man!" said Mr. Chow, the fortuneteller. "He had better stick to his rattraps!" And then he turned with a bow to the Mandarin. "My sons and I will make the kite you ask for."

The Mandarin tugged thoughtfully at his wispy beard. "We shall see. Whoever makes a festival kite that most suits my fancy will join my court as official maker of kites."

When Grandfather returned, Miss Singsong told him the news. He gave a snort at the mention of Mr. Chow and his four sons. "They make kites that insult the skies," he said. "They make kites as ugly as themselves!"

"Then you will try?" Miss Singsong asked anxiously.

"I will try."

For a week Grandfather did not stir from the village. He chose the finest bamboo and silk. Day by day he shaped the wings and the delicate body and the flaring tail. A second week passed, for Grandfather would not be hurried.

And then it was the third day of the ninth

moon. Mr. Chow and his sons proudly carried their finished kite to the Mandarin. It had the look of the Thing-in-the-Sky, though the wings were set a bit crooked and the tail drooped.

But it took lightly to the air and Miss Sing-song's heart dropped. The Mandarin would be satisfied, she thought. On the ninth day he would fly it in the Festival of Kites. He would match it against the kites of other lords and strut about in a proud manner.

She turned away from the sky. The Mandarin was standing with his legs apart, and she was surprised to see a look of rage in his eyes.

"Fools!" he shouted furiously. "Where is the angry noise?"

"Noise?" said Mr. Chow, startled.

"Were you deaf? Didn't you hear the foreign toy roar and sing and hum in the sky? Why doesn't your kite do the same?"

Each day after that, Mr. Chow and his sons could be seen testing their kite on the wind. They attached hollow bamboo sticks meant to roar in the sky. But they only whistled. They attached wire strings meant to sing. But they only moaned. They attached paper streamers

meant to hum. But they only flapped and crackled.

"The Mandarin asks the impossible!" Mr. Chow growled and groaned.

Meanwhile, Grandfather put the finishing touches on his own kite. Miss Singsong helped him stretch silk over the great soaring wings and slim body and the finlike tail. It was becoming as beautiful as a dragonfly, she thought.

But Grandfather's Thing-in-the-Sky would not make angry sounds either. It would not roar and sing and hum on the wind. The Mandarin would shake with disappointment and rage. And Grandfather would have to return to his springs and blocks of wood — his wooden cats.

She lay awake most of the night while Grandfather worked. If only she could think of a way to give the kite its voice.

And then the ninth day of the ninth moon arrived.

The sun rose, bobbing like a cork on the South China Sea. Roosters crowed. When the Mandarin awoke and looked out his window he saw a Thing-in-the-Sky.

He hurried through his gardens and out of the moon gate. He kept his eyes lifted, gazing at the kite floating gracefully in the breeze. Its wings were as evenly set as a bird's. Its tail was straight. And best of all, it hummed away angrily.

The Mandarin beamed. Here was the kite he had dreamed of! Here was the kite for a mandarin on festival day!

Miss Singsong helped Grandfather hold fast to the kite string. Her heart beat a little faster as she saw the Mandarin bear down on them. Hearing the noise in the sky, villagers flew from their houses. Mr. Chow and his four sons raised their eyes and glared.

"You are The Wooden Cat Man, eh?" said the Mandarin.

Grandfather nodded.

"Your kite *hums* — but does it *sing*?"

Grandfather let out more string. As the kite rose higher among the clouds, the hum faded into a distant singing sound.

The Mandarin smiled and pulled at his wispy beard.

"Your kite *sings* — but does it *roar*?" he asked.

Together Grandfather and Miss Singsong pulled in the string. As the kite was plucked out of the clouds and drew near, it gave off a roar.

The Mandarin clucked his tongue with pleasure and slipped his hands into his sleeves. "You will make wooden cats no longer," he announced. "You will join my court as maker of kites!"

Miss Singsong could hardly refrain from leaping with joy. Wasn't Grandfather a great artist? He would be able to spend all his days making beautiful kites in the shapes of dragons and butterflies and frogs and fish. The Mandarin's kites — *his* kites — would be famous all over China.

Grandfather and Miss Singsong continued winding in the string. The Mandarin shook his head in wonder. "Maker of kites," he said.

"What makes your kite hum and sing and roar, eh?"

Smiling, Grandfather turned a proud eye on Miss Singsong. "It was my granddaughter's idea," he said.

The kite landed as gently as a leaf on the field. Everyone rushed toward it.

And they saw that the inside of the kite was painted with fresh honey sprinkled with fresh orange blossoms. And they saw that the inside of the kite was swarming with bees.

"Bees!" the Mandarin laughed. "Bees feasting on honey and the nectar of orange blossoms. Imagine!"

Mr. Chow and his sons groaned, and stormed away.

The Mandarin, still chuckling, made a bow toward Miss Singsong. "Bees. A swarm of bees. Imagine!"

She bowed in return. She thought back to the day when the Thing-in-the-Sky had first appeared. It might not have been golden, with the tail of a peacock, but she would always think of it as the *fung-hwang* — the bird of good luck, the bringer of good fortune.

What good luck, she thought, that she had stepped on a bee!

AUTHOR

Born in Brooklyn, New York, Sid Fleischman grew up in California. He had always been interested in magic, and he wrote a book about magic when he was seventeen years old. He then worked as a magician for a traveling magic show to pay his way through college.

Mr. Fleischman and his wife and three children live in San Diego, California, where he once worked as a newspaper reporter. He has written books for adults as well as children and has won a number of awards. For example, *By the Great Horn Spoon!* was chosen best book of its year by the Boys Clubs of America. Other books by Mr. Fleischman include *The Ghost in the Noonday Sun, Longbeard the Wizard, Mr. Mysterious and Company,* and the popular *McBroom* series. He says, "Writing *Mr. Mysterious* was a special treat. As I finished each chapter I read it to my children. When I couldn't figure out what was to happen next, I asked them for ideas."

Maria Mitchell

by Katharine E. Wilkie

Maria Mitchell was born on the island of Nantucket, Massachusetts, in 1818. Her family were Quakers, and her father was an astronomer. From the time Maria was a little girl, she loved to go up to the rooftop with her father. Together they would watch the stars and planets through a telescope. Maria learned so much about astronomy that she became her father's official helper when she was only twelve.

In those days, many people thought girls should not be interested in astronomy and other sciences. But the Nantucket Quakers like the Mitchells were strong-minded people. They did what they thought was right, even when their ideas seemed strange to others.

This story is from the book, *Maria Mitchell: Stargazer,* by Katharine E. Wilkie. The story begins on the night of October 1, 1847. At this time, Maria was a young woman working at the Atheneum Library on Nantucket.

It had been a long day at the Atheneum. Maria found a half-dozen guests in the parlor when she returned to her home. She soon left them and slipped away to the housetop. It was a perfect autumn night for sweeping the skies.

Maria turned the telescope to look at the constellation Orion. Then through the lens she sighted the star group called the Corona Borealis. Downstairs Maria could hear laughter and talking, but she was glad to be up here alone with the stars.

Suddenly Maria stiffened. There in the upper part of the view through the telescope was a tiny white spot. She knew that part of the heavens as well as she knew the Atheneum. No white spot should be there. She turned her head and closed her eyes. Could her eyes be tricking her?

Again she looked through the lens. The white spot was still there.

The chronometer showed that the time was exactly half past ten. She wrote down the figures and hurried down the narrow attic stairs to find her father. She must be sure!

The guests stopped talking as she rushed into the room. Mr. Mitchell looked up.

"Come quickly, Father!" begged Maria.

She turned and flew back up the stairs with her father close behind. Her mother, her sister Kate, and the guests followed.

Up on the rooftop William Mitchell looked carefully through the lens. He shook his head and turned away. Then he looked again for a long time. With a proud smile he turned to the others and spoke.

"My friends, I believe my daughter has discovered a new comet!"

That night Mr. Mitchell wrote to his old friend, Professor Bond, at Harvard University. Before long a letter from the professor arrived. He had used Maria's reckoning and found the comet with his telescope.

Father waved the letter. "I *told* thee! Soon the whole world will be hearing of thy comet."

"Do not call it *my* comet," Maria answered.

"Why not? A comet is always named for the person who discovers it. Thee will soon be hearing more. Professor Bond has sent a notice to a German journal which announces all such discoveries."

Day after day passed. At last Maria's father had another letter.

"Just listen to this!" he exclaimed. "Professor Bond writes: 'It seems that Maria Mitchell's comet has not been seen before in Europe.' He looked proudly at his daughter. "Twenty-nine years old, and already you have become a famous astronomer!"

"Thee has taught me all I know," Maria told him. "It is as much thy discovery as mine."

In 1831 the King of Denmark had promised a gold medal to the first person

to discover a "telescopic comet." This kind of comet is visible only through a telescope.

Was Maria the first to announce the discovery of the comet? There seemed to be some doubt. Because of a storm, the ship carrying her father's letter did not leave Nantucket until three days after Maria's discovery. A man in Rome had seen the comet on October 3. Who had announced it first?

Many important people were drawn into the question. At last, on October 6, 1848, the King of Denmark awarded the medal to Maria.

"Now thee is beginning thy career," William Mitchell told her.

Maria shook her head. "I began it long ago when thee first taught me the wonder of the stars."

———

It was 1857, nine years after Maria had received the medal from the King of Denmark. That honor had brought her fame. She had continued to do outstanding work in astronomy. Now she was going to Europe.

Maria left Nantucket in a shower of good wishes. Wonderful days lay ahead, and Maria enjoyed every moment of them. In England Maria visited the homes of authors whose works she had read and loved. She even tracked down the old home

of Isaac Newton, the famous scientist who had discovered the laws of gravity.

It was hard for Maria to realize that she herself was famous. All the leading British scientists wanted to meet her.

From England Maria went to France and then to Italy. She was enchanted by Rome, and her greatest wish was to visit the Vatican Observatory there. No woman had ever been there. But Maria asked permission and received it.

"You never get anything if you don't ask for it," she said with simple New England frankness.

It was a thrilling moment when she stood in the Observatory. It was here that the famous Galileo had been on trial over two hundred years before. In Galileo's day, most people believed that the earth was the center of everything. They felt it was a crime to think otherwise. Galileo had said that the earth and the other planets

The Maria Mitchell House, Nantucket, Massachusetts

revolve around the sun. He had been forced to deny his belief, even though he was later proved right.

Maria Mitchell returned home and taught for many years at Vassar College in the state of New York. Even after she had retired from teaching, she continued her work in astronomy.

Today visitors come from all over the world to the Maria Mitchell Museum on Nantucket Island. It was once the gray-shingled home of a Quaker child who wondered about everything in the world, especially the stars, and who grew up to be the first woman astronomer in America.

AUTHOR

Katherine Wilkie is a native of Kentucky. She was born in Lexington and went to the University of Kentucky in that city, where she met her husband. After they finished college, the Wilkies decided to stay in Lexington.

Mrs. Wilkie has written several books about famous people besides Maria Mitchell. Some of her books are:

Daniel Boone: Taming the Wilds

Mary Todd Lincoln, Girl of the Bluegrass

William Penn: Friend to All

Helen Keller: Handicapped Girl

Pocahontas: Indian Princess

Mrs. Wilkie is a seventh-grade teacher, and she also writes books for teenagers.

A Picture Puzzle

The name NINA is hidden in this picture five times. How many NINAs can *you* find?

For many years, people enjoyed finding the NINAs in Al Hirschfeld's picture puzzles. In this one, Mr. Hirschfeld pictured three popular old-time movie comedians, the Marx Brothers.

Autumn Thought

Flowers are happy in summer.
In autumn they die and are blown away.
  Dry and withered,
Their petals dance on the wind
Like little brown butterflies.

– Langston Hughes

Skill

Lesson:

RECOGNIZING THE POWER OF WORDS

Words are really wonderful things. Sometimes they help us to paint a picture in our minds, and they can also make us feel happy or sad. People who write stories or poems choose words that help us to understand their feelings about places, people, or things.

Each numbered sentence below is what someone might write to describe a fog that was closing in around him or her. Can you see any difference in the words which have been chosen to describe the fog?

1. I could see less and less as a thick fog came up around me.
2. Slowly, slowly, the fog rolled nearer and nearer, until it brushed my cheeks and erased all the trees and earth around me.

3. The fog crept in as silently as a shadow, spreading its web-like curtain on the walls of the sky, and I was caught in its silk cocoon.

What word is used in Sentence 1 to describe the fog?

Sentence 2 uses words that tell how slowly the fog comes near to the person, and how close and really thick it is.

Sentence 3 uses very different words to describe the coming of the fog. Notice that, unlike the other two sentences, it gives some idea as to how the person felt. Can you find the metaphors and similes in Sentences 2 and 3?

An author uses words in different ways to get you to feel something about what he or she is saying. We call these words **descriptive words.** Descriptive words are something like words that help you to paint a picture in your mind. But many times descriptive words help you to do more than just *see* such a picture. They can help you *feel,* or even *smell, taste,* or *hear* what the author is talking about.

Discussion

Help your class answer these questions:
1. What words in Sentence 1 describe the fog and tell you where it is?

2. What words in Sentence 2 does the author use to tell you that the fog is very, very close to the person?

3. When the author says, in Sentence 2, that the fog "erased all the trees and earth around me," what does that mean to you? What happens when you erase something? Were the trees and earth *really* erased? How are the words *brushed* and *erased* both metaphors?

4. What do the words "crept in as silently as a shadow" tell you about the fog? What is the simile in those words? What other simile is there in Sentence 3?

5. In Sentence 3, what is the fog being compared to by the metaphor, "was spreading its web-like curtain on the walls of the sky"?

6. Why is "I was caught in its silk cocoon" a metaphor?

On your own

As you read the following two paragraphs to yourself, notice the words that are used to describe how the puppy *felt*. What do the other words help you to see or hear?

The puppy was very sad. He sat alone on the steps. He didn't have anyone to play with.

Then two boys came along. The puppy chased

them. They made a lot of noise. They all fell down in a heap.

Now read the next two paragraphs about the same puppy, and try to decide why the two stories about the same thing are really quite different. As you read, notice the words that are used to make you feel happy or sad or lonely, and those that help you see and hear what was happening.

It was an unhappy picture. The poor little puppy sat all alone at the foot of the steps . . . as if he didn't have a friend in the whole wide world. His sad brown eyes seemed to be pleading for someone to come to talk or to play with him. One ear drooped like a wet dishrag, and he slumped his body down as if his legs could never lift his load of sadness. The only sound to be heard was the steady buzz of a fly that circled the puppy's head. The dog didn't move or blink an eye. He just sat —a lonely lump of sadness.

Suddenly, around the corner of the house two boys came flying, one behind the other. The "wet dishrag" perked up, the eyes shone, the limp legs stiffened and pushed the body into motion, and the puppy took off in wild chase. The noise was deafening. The air was filled with shouts, and barks, and laughter, all tangled in a pile of arms and legs and a thumping, wagging puppy tail.

Checking your work

If you are asked to do so, compare the feelings you had as you read the second pair of paragraphs with those you had as you read the first pair. With your class, decide what words or groups of words in the second pair of paragraphs helped you most to feel just how sad and lonely the puppy was and then how excited he became later. You may want to make a list of them. Then decide what words or groups of words helped you most to imagine what you would have seen and heard if you had been there.

A Joke

Mr. See: I fell over fifty feet this morning.

Mr. Saw: Fifty feet! Weren't you hurt?

Mr. See: No, I was just walking through a crowded bus.

COPLAS

People in villages in Spain often make up and sing short songs called *coplas*. These little folk songs can be about many different things. Here are some examples:

Tengo mi pecho de coplas,
Que parece un hormiguero;
Y unas a otras se dicen:
¡Yo quiero salir primero!

Al subir por la escalera,
Una pulga me picó,
La cogí de las orejas . . .
¡Buen puntapié me dio!

Aunque te digan pecosa,
Niña, no te sepa malo;
Que el cielo con sus estrellas
Está muy bien adornado.

Mira el cielo vestirse
De ricas telas,
De día, azul y blanco,
De noche, estrellas.

My heart is filled with coplas,
Like a swarming anthill;
And each says to the other:
Let me out first!

As I climbed the stairs
A flea did bite me,
I caught it by the ears . . .
But what a kick it gave me!

Though they call you freckles,
Don't be insulted;
The sky with its stars
Is amply speckled.

See how the sky dresses
In rich fabric,
By day it wears white and blue,
At night, stars.

Annie and the Old One

by Miska Miles

Annie's Navajo world was good — a world of rippling sand, of high copper-red bluffs in the distance, of the low mesa near her own snug hogan. The pumpkins were yellow in the cornfield, and the tassels on the corn were turning brown.

Each morning, the gate to the night pen near the hogan was opened wide and the sheep were herded to pasture on the desert.

Annie helped watch the sheep. She carried pails of water to the cornfield. And every weekday, she walked to the bus stop and waited for the yellow bus that took her to school and brought her home again.

Adapted from *Annie and the Old One* by Miska Miles. Published by Little, Brown and Company.

Best of all were the evenings when she sat at her grandmother's feet and listened to stories of times long gone.

Sometimes it seemed to Annie that her grandmother was her age — a girl who had seen no more than nine or ten harvestings.

If a mouse scurried and jerked across the hard dirt floor of their hogan, Annie and her grandmother laughed together. And when they prepared the fried bread for the evening meal, if it burned a bit black at the edges, they laughed and said it was good.

There were other times when her grandmother sat small and still, and Annie knew that she was very old. Then Annie would cover the thin knees of the Old One with a warm blanket.

It was at such a time that her grandmother

said, "It is time you learn to weave, my grand-daughter."

Annie touched the web of wrinkles that criss-crossed her grandmother's face and slowly went outside the hogan.

Beside the door, her father sat cross-legged, working with silver and fire, making a handsome, heavy necklace. Annie passed him and went to the big loom where her mother sat weaving.

Annie sat beside the loom, watching, while her mother slid the weaving stick in place among the strings of the warp. With red wool, her mother added a row to a slanting arrow of red, bright against the dull background.

Annie's thoughts wandered. She thought about the stories her grandmother had told — stories of hardship when rains flooded the desert — of dry weather when rains did not fall and the pumpkins and corn were dry in the field.

Annie looked out across the sand where the cactus bore its red fruit, and thought about the coyote guarding the scattered hogans of the Navajos.

Annie watched while her mother worked. She made herself sit very still.

clear music of the bell on the collar of the lead goat.

The weaving of the rug was high on the loom. It was almost as high as Annie's waist.

"My mother," Annie said, "why do you weave?"

"I weave so we may sell the rug and buy the things we must have from the trading post. Silver for silvermaking. Deer hide for boots —"

"But you know what my grandmother said —"

Annie's mother did not speak. She slid her weaving stick through the warp and picked up a strand of rose-red wool.

Annie turned and ran. She ran across the sand and huddled in the shade of the small mesa. Her grandmother would go back to the earth when the rug was taken from the loom. The rug must not be finished. Her mother must not weave.

A Part of the Earth

The next morning, where her grandmother went, Annie followed.

When it was time to go to the bus stop to meet the school bus, she dawdled, walking slowly and watching her feet. Perhaps she would miss the bus.

And then quite suddenly she did not want to miss it. She knew what she must do.

She ran hard, as fast as she could — breathing deeply — and the yellow bus was waiting for her at the stop.

She climbed aboard. The bus moved on, stopping now and then at hogans along the way. Annie sat there alone and made her plan.

In school, she would be bad, so bad that the teacher would send for her mother and father.

And if her mother and father came to school to talk to the teacher, that would be one day her mother could not weave. One day.

On the playground, Annie's teacher asked, "Who will lead the exercises today?"

No one answered.

The teacher laughed, "Very well. Then I shall be leader." The teacher was young, with yellow hair. Her blue skirt was wide and the heels on her brown shoes were high. The teacher kicked off her shoes and the girls laughed.

Annie followed the teacher's lead — bending, jumping, and she waited for the time when the teacher would lead them in jogging around the playground.

As Annie jogged past the spot where the teacher's shoes lay on the ground, she picked up a shoe and hid it in the folds of her dress.

And when Annie jogged past a trash can, she dropped the shoe inside.

Some of the girls saw her and laughed, but some frowned. When the line jogged near the schoolhouse door, Annie slipped from the line and went inside to her room and her own desk.

Clearly she heard the teacher as she spoke to the girls outside.

"The other shoe, please." Her voice was pleasant. There was silence.

Limping, one shoe on and one shoe gone, the teacher came into the room.

The girls followed, giggling and holding their hands across their mouths.

"I know it's funny," the teacher said, "but now I need the shoe."

Annie looked at the boards of the floor. A shiny black beetle crawled between the cracks.

The door opened and a man teacher came inside with a shoe in his hand. As he passed Annie's desk, he touched her shoulder and smiled down at her.

"I saw someone playing tricks," he said.

The teacher looked at Annie and the room was very still.

When school was over for the day, Annie waited.

Timidly, with hammering heart, she went to the teacher's desk.

"Do you want my mother and father to come to the school tomorrow?" she asked.

"No, Annie," the teacher said. "I have the shoe. Everything is all right."

Annie's face was hot and her hands were cold. She turned and ran. She was the last to climb on the bus.

Finally, there was her own bus stop. She hopped down and slowly trudged the long way home. She stopped beside the loom.

The rug was now much higher than her waist.

That night she curled up in her blanket. She slept lightly, and awakened before dawn.

There was no sound from her mother's sheepskin. Her grandmother was a quiet hump in her blanket. Annie heard only her father's loud, sleeping breathing. There was no other sound on the whole earth, except the howling of a coyote from far across the desert.

In the dim light of early morning, Annie crept outside to the night pen where the sheep were sleeping. The dry wood creaked when she opened the gate and pushed it wide open.

She tugged at the sleeping sheep until one stood quietly. Then the others stood also, uncertain — shoving together. The lead goat turned toward the open gate and Annie slipped her fingers through his belled collar. She curled her fingertips across the bell, muffling its sound, and led the goat through the gate. The sheep followed.

She led them across the sand and around the small mesa where she released the goat.

"Go," she said.

She ran back to the hogan, and slid under her blanket and lay shivering. Now her family would hunt the sheep all day. This would be the day when her mother would not weave.

When the fullness of morning came and it was light, Annie watched her grandmother rise and go outside.

Annie heard her call.

"The sheep are gone."

Annie's mother and father hurried outside and Annie followed.

Her mother moaned softly, "The sheep — the sheep —"

"I see them," the grandmother said. "They graze near the mesa."

Annie went with her grandmother and when they reached the sheep, Annie's fingers slipped under the goat's collar and the bell tinkled sharply as the sheep followed back to the pen.

In school that day, Annie sat quietly and wondered what more she could do. When the teacher asked questions, Annie looked at the floor. She did not even hear.

When night came, she curled up in her blanket, but not to sleep.

When everything was still, she slipped from her blanket and crept outside.

The sky was dark and secret. The wind was soft against her face. For a moment she stood waiting until she could see in the night. She went to the loom.

She felt for the weaving stick there in its place among the warp strings. She separated the warp and felt for the wool.

Slowly she pulled out the strands of yarn, one by one.

One by one, she laid them across her knees.

And when the row was removed, she separated

the strings of the warp again, and reached for the second row.

When the woven rug was only as high as her waist, she crept back to her blanket, taking the strands of wool with her.

Under the blanket, she smoothed the strands and made them into a ball. And then she slept.

The next night, Annie removed another day's weaving. In the morning when her mother went to the loom, she looked at the weaving — puzzled —

For a moment, she pressed her fingers against her eyes.

The Old One looked at Annie curiously. Annie held her breath.

The third night, Annie crept to the loom.

A gentle hand touched her shoulder.

"Go to sleep, my granddaughter," the Old One said.

Annie wanted to throw her arms around her grandmother's waist and tell her why she had been bad, but she could only stumble to her blanket and huddle under it and let the tears roll into the edge of her hair.

When morning came, Annie unrolled herself from the blanket and helped prepare the morning meal.

Afterward, she followed her grandmother through the cornfield. Her grandmother walked slowly, and Annie fitted her steps to the slow steps of the Old One.

When they reached the small mesa, the Old One sat crossing her knees, folding her gnarled fingers into her lap.

Annie knelt beside her.

The Old One looked far off toward the rim of desert where sky met sand.

"My granddaughter," she said, "you have

tried to hold back time. This cannot be done."
The desert stretched yellow and brown away to
the edge of the morning sky. "The sun comes up
from the edge of earth in the morning. It returns
to the edge of earth in the evening. Earth, from
which good things come for the living creatures
on it. Earth, to which all creatures finally go."

Annie picked up a handful of brown sand and
pressed it against the palm of her hand. Slowly,
she let it fall to earth. She understood many
things.

The sun rose but it also set.

The cactus did not bloom forever. Petals dried
and fell to earth.

She knew that she was a part of the earth and
the things in it. She would always be a part of
the earth, just as her grandmother had always
been, just as her grandmother would always be,
always and forever.

And Annie was breathless with the wonder of it.

They walked back to the hogan together, Annie and the Old One.

Annie picked up the old weaving stick.

"I am ready to weave," she said to her mother. "I will use the stick that my grandmother has given me." She knelt at the loom.

She separated the warp strings and slipped the weaving stick in place, as her mother had done, as her grandmother had done.

She picked up a strand of gray wool and started to weave.

AUTHOR

Miska Miles is a pen name that Patricia Miles Martin often uses. This author has written many books under both her real name and her pen name. She is not only an author of stories for young people but is a teacher and poet as well. She also has a rather unusual hobby: collecting kerosene lamps.

Mrs. Martin has received many honors for her writing. For example, *The Pointed Brush* was chosen an Honor Book by the New York *Herald Tribune* newspaper. *Kickapoo,* written under the name Miska Miles, was a Junior Literary Guild selection. Mrs. Martin writes several different types of books: biographies, fiction, and non-fiction. Some books under the name Miska Miles are *The Pieces of Home, Wharf Rat,* and *Mississippi Possum.* Under her real name, Patricia Miles Martin, are many more, such as *Jump Frog Jump, Chicanos,* and *John Fitzgerald Kennedy.*

Dance of the Animals

a Puerto Rican folktale by Pura Belpré

Once upon a time, a Lion and a Lioness lived together near a great forest and had for neighbors such couples as Señor Horse and Señora Mare, Señor and Señora Donkey, Señor Bull and Señora Cow, Señor and Señora Dog, and Señor and Señora Goat.

Times were bad for them, and soon the day came when they faced each other with nothing in the house to mix for a meal.

"We must do something," said the Lioness. "If times keep up like this, we shall certainly perish, a thing which should not happen, for are we not the strongest beasts in the forest? Has it not been said that the biggest fish shall eat the smaller?"

"True enough," answered the Lion. "Something must be done." And he set to thinking for a while.

"I have it," said he, after a while, "and a splendid idea it is, even if I have to say it myself! Listen. Which meat do we like the best?"

"Goat's meat," answered Señora Lioness.

"Right," said the Lion. "It is the finest, the juiciest, and certainly the tastiest."

"Ah, *Señora mía,* you shall see," explained the Lion.

"But how are we going to get such fresh and delicious meat?" asked the Lioness. "To hear you talk, one would think we are kings."

"I will tell you," said Señor Lion. "Listen carefully. We shall give a ball, a grand ball, and to it we shall invite our friends. You who are so well liked will invite our neighbors, and they will not refuse. Outside the back door we will build a fire. When the dance begins and everyone is on the floor, I will push the goat and cast him into the fire. The rest depends on me. How do you like my plan?"

Señora Lioness thought for a while, shaking her head slowly at first as if the plan did not meet with her approval. Then, suddenly realizing what it all meant, she exclaimed, "Oh, most generous idea! Meat at last."

"You will have to hurry if my plans are to be carried out," said Señor Lion.

Señora Lioness went out to invite the neighbors, while Señor Lion stayed home to prepare the house for the big affair.

"*Hola!* Señora Mare," exclaimed Señora Lioness, as she came upon her in the forest.

"*Hola!* Señora Lioness! What are you doing around these parts, my good friend?"

"I came to invite you to a dance at our house. You and Señor Horse have such fine long legs and such strong hoofs. We need you for our orchestra. Could you not come and play the drum?"

"Oh, most certainly," answered Señora Mare. "Only yesterday was I saying that we needed a little recreation. Yes, we will come and play the drum!"

"*Gracias*," said Señora Lioness and went her way.

Pretty soon she found Señora Donkey.

"Ah, *amiga mía*," said she, greeting her friend. "I was just going to your house. We are giving a ball and would like to have you and Señor Donkey come. Señor Horse and Señora Mare are coming to play the drum. Won't you and Señor Donkey come and play the trombone?"

"Why, yes, Señora Lioness, we will be there without fail."

"*Gracias! Gracias!*" said Señora Lioness. "You see your voices are so rich that without their resonance our ball would be a failure . . ."

On went Señora Lioness, faster and faster as she felt the pangs of hunger in her empty stomach. She had not had goat's meat in such a long time. She crossed lane after lane inviting here and there, and giving each invitation with such graciousness that those invited felt that the dance would not be a success unless they accepted.

When she reached Señora Dog's house, she found them sitting under the shade of a great tree.

"*Hola amigos!*" cried she, a little breathless,

for she had walked quite a distance now and
her throat was beginning to feel dry after so
much talking.

"There is a great ball at my house tonight.
You must both come," said Señora Lioness.

"I will go," said the dog, "but Señora Dog
stays home."

"I will go, too," said Señora Dog quickly.

"No, no," shrieked Señor Dog.

"*Sí, sí,*" yelled Señora Dog.

"Oh, my friends," said Señora Lioness, hurriedly, "I must leave you to decide the matter
yourselves. I must call at Señor Goat's house."

"Wait, Señora Lioness! Señor Goat is my best
friend. I will take you there," said Señor Dog.

Once at Señor Goat's house, Señor Dog drew him aside and suggested that he should go alone to the dance.

It was done as he said. So Señora Dog and Señora Goat missed Señora Lioness's ball.

Señora Lioness left with a sad heart, for Señor Goat would not render enough meat for two.

Why did she have to invite the dog first? Why didn't she ignore him just this once? What would Señor Lion say when he heard that only Señor Goat was coming? Señor Goat, so thin and lanky!

She soon reached home. Señor Lion had straightened things, and outside the door a large bonfire flared. On a tripod hung a large earthenware pot. Señora Lioness heard the water sizzle and reach the boiling point. She hurried in.

"Well, you are here at last," cried the Lion. "Are they all coming?"

"Yes, all — that is, except — "

She never finished the sentence, for so excited was Señor Lion that he danced around the house for joy and then went out to tend the fire.

Señora Lioness had hardly finished placing a

garland of coffee flowers on her neck when the first guests arrived.

"*Buenos días*," said she, greeting Señor and Señora Donkey. The newcomers looked spotlessly clean, and in order to play freely they had refrained from wearing ornaments.

"What a beautiful garland!" exclaimed Señor Donkey. "And how becoming!"

"*Gracias,* my friend," answered Señora Lioness.

Another pair came along. This time it was Señor and Señora Cat.

"Oh!" exclaimed Señora Lioness, a note of admiration in her voice. "What an adorable necklace!"

Señora Cat had woven honeysuckle and pinned a bunch around her neck on a blue ribbon. She looked like a flower herself, her beautiful eyes dancing for pure joy. Her white fur stood out as if it had been freshly brushed. As she moved about, the delicate scent of honeysuckle spread, perfuming the air.

When Señor Bull and Señora Cow appeared, they were as pretty as a picture. From the river they came, yet dry and shining! They had

threaded gray and red chaplets around their
horns. The tan of their hides had a lustrous
shine and the gray and red of the berries stood
out against the black of their large soft eyes.

Last came Señor Dog and Señor Goat.

"And the Señoras?" inquired Señor Lion.
"Aren't they coming?"

"No," said Señor Goat.

"Oh no!" said Señor Dog.

"My dear," whispered Señor Lion to Señora
Lioness, "we shall have to eat them both, since
Señora Goat did not come."

Like Señor and Señora Donkey, Señor Goat
and Señor Dog wore no ornaments; but their
guilt in leaving their respective wives home
showed in their faces.

Motioning to the orchestra to begin, Señor Lion and Señora Lioness opened the dance. The couples whirled, stamped, and bellowed. What tangoes and *jotas*! Waltzes mingled with mazurkas and traditional dances. And the orchestra! Never had there been one like it! Señora Ant played the guitar. The drum was placed in such a convenient place that Señor Horse had no difficulty in striking it with his hoofs, as he danced around.

What a resonance! Señor Dog barked and howled. Señor and Señora Cat miaowed, while the constant stamping of Señor Donkey and the bombarding brays of Señora Mare filled the place. On and on the couples danced until the floor creaked under the weight of their bodies.

Suddenly on one of the turns of a dance Señor Goat and Señor Dog, who for lack of partners were dancing together, spied the bonfire outside the door.

"*Amigo*," said the goat, "I do not like the look of that fire. Let us go, for this bonfire is meant for us and so is the pot of boiling water hanging over it. No doubt, Señor Lion means to eat us up."

Through the dancing couples they pulled and pushed, skipping all the time until they reached the farther door. Once out, they ran as fast as their legs could carry them, looking back now and then to see if they were being followed.

Meanwhile, at the ball, things went on as before. Suddenly Señor Lion missed Señor Dog and Señor Goat. As quickly as he could, without causing suspicion, he left the house.

The afternoon was cool and the air was heavy with the scent of the acacia trees in full bloom. The wind began to blow and with it a sprinkle of rain, which came slowly at first and then in great torrents. On and on ran Señor Lion and, coming out at the turn of the road, he spied Señor Dog and Señor Goat, running ahead of him. Faster and faster ran the Lion, yet faster went Señor Dog and Señor Goat.

They soon reached the river. It was swollen with the sudden downpour. The dog was not afraid and swam across, but the goat did not know what to do. Looking back he saw Señor Lion coming closer and closer.

"Oh, for a good place of safety!" he said.

As he turned around, he spied a large bunch of hay. He quickly got under it and rolled himself until only his tail stuck out. Presently Señor Lion reached the shore.

"Where have they gone?" exclaimed he. He
heard a sharp call. He looked across the river and
there he saw Señor Dog happily jumping and
mocking him. Señor Lion snarled and showed
his fangs. If he could only swim across, he
thought, he could show this impudent dog what
he could do. But he could not and, what was
more humiliating, Señor Dog knew it, too.

"You are so clever and quick," called the dog
across the river. "Why don't you swim? Surely
the current will help you."

Señor Lion was furious. Swim indeed!

"I'll make your babbling tongue stop," he
called back.

He looked around. The place was full of
stones. He picked up one and hurled it at the

dog across the river. Señor Dog saw it coming and jumped out of reach.

"Oh, my friend," he called, "see the bundle of straw near you? Why don't you try and throw a stalk of that at me?"

"One stalk, indeed," roared Señor Lion, fully realizing that Señor Dog was making fun of his strength. "I will throw you the pack."

So saying he leaned forward and tried to pull at the pack, which, besides being slippery because of the rain, was quite heavy with the weight of the goat inside of it. No sooner had he pulled at it than he slipped and fell on his back.

At this Señor Dog leaped up and barked for

joy. "Try again, my friend," he called at Señor Lion.

Señor Lion stood up and went at the straw pack again. He pulled and pulled and, finally raising it, he hurled it across the river. No sooner did it land on the ground than Señor Goat jumped out of his hiding place and, accompanied by Señor Dog, began to cut capers in the air.

"Señor Lion," he called, "thanks for ferrying me over. If I did lose my tail, my life indeed I saved!"

Señor Lion's rage had no limit and, looking down at his paws, he discovered that he had a large amount of fur entangled in his claws. Then he laughed and answered:

"So you have, my friend, but by your stump you'll tell your tale."

And it is true, because even to this day, goats have only a stump for a tail.

AUTHOR

"Storytelling was a natural pastime as I grew up in Puerto Rico," says Pura Belpré (poo'rah bell'pray). The old Puerto Rican folktales, which she heard told and retold often in her childhood, were to become very important to her in her later work.

When she was a young woman, Pura Belpré came from Puerto Rico to New York to attend her sister's wedding. At that time she decided to stay in New York and go to library school. She later became a children's librarian and married Clarence Cameron White, a well-known musician. Now a widow, she still lives in New York and has been a librarian and storyteller in all parts of the city.

Pura Belpré's first book was published because of some homework she did at library school. Each person in her storytelling class had to write down an old folktale. She chose *Perez and Martina,* a story that her grandmother had often told her in Puerto Rico. Another student in the class worked for a publishing company. He liked the story so much that he persuaded his company to publish it as a book.

When Pura Belpré tells stories to children, she uses puppets to make the stories even more enjoyable. From the time she was a child, she has always been interested in puppets. Even before she ever saw any real puppets, she was making her own out of fruit, or whatever else was around at home.

Pura Belpré's storytelling has not only been fun for New York children, but it has been valuable as well. She of course speaks Spanish as well as English. Because of this, she has been very helpful to Spanish-speaking newcomers to New York from Puerto Rico and other countries. She often tells them familiar stories, in Spanish, to make them feel at home in their new land.

Dance of the Animals is from *The Tiger and the Rabbit and Other Tales,* and the story has also been published as a separate picture book. Other books by Pura Belpré are *Santiago, Juan Bobo and the Queen's Necklace,* and *Ote: A Puerto Rican Folk Tale.* In all her work, her purpose has been to share with all children, through folk literature, the rich cultural heritage of Puerto Rico.

BOOKS TO ENJOY

THE TALES OF OLGA DA POLGA *by Michael Bond*

Olga is a talented, talkative pet guinea pig. Her funny tales explain such things as why guinea pigs squeak and why they have no tails.

OWLET, THE GREAT HORNED OWL *by Irene Brady*

In this beautifully illustrated life story, Owlet proves that he can defend himself in the dangerous woods.

THE YEAR MOM WON THE PENNANT

by Matt Christopher

When Nick's Little League baseball team needs a new coach, his mother volunteers for the job — with some surprising results.

GERTRUDE'S POCKET *by Miska Miles*

After a fight with the school bully, an Appalachian girl makes good use of the dollar she carries in her pocket.

THE GOOD GUYS AND THE BAD GUYS

by Osmond Molarsky

Doug and Parker track down the roller-skate thief in their big-city neighborhood.

TALKING DRUMS OF AFRICA *by Christine Price*

This book explains how African drums are made and how they can speak, sing, and tell stories.

LANGSTON HUGHES *by Alice Walker*

Here is a fine, short biography of a man who is famous for the many kinds of books he wrote, both for children and adults.

GLOSSARY

This glossary can help you find out meanings and pronunciations of words in this book that you may not know. The meanings of the words as they are used in this book are always given. Often you will also find other common meanings listed.

You can find out the correct pronunciation of any glossary word by using the special spelling after the word and the pronunciation key. The *Full Pronunciation Key* below shows how to pronounce each consonant and vowel in a special spelling. There is also a short form of this full key at the bottom of every left-hand page in the glossary.

Full Pronunciation Key

Consonant Sounds

/b/	bib	/k/	cat, kick	/sh/	ship, dish
/ch/	church	/l/	lid, needle	/t/	tight
/d/	did	/m/	man, am	/th/	thin, path
/f/	fast, off	/n/	no, sudden	/*th*/	this, bathe
/g/	gag	/ng/	thing	/v/	vine, cave
/h/	hat	/p/	pop	/w/	with
/hw/	which	/r/	roar	/y/	yes
/j/	judge	/s/	see, miss	/z/	zebra, size
				/zh/	pleasure

Vowel Sounds

/ă/	pat	/ĭ/	pit	/oi/	noise, boy
/ā/	pay	/ī/	pie, by	/ou/	out, cow
/â/	air, care	/î/	fierce, dear	/o͝o/	took
/ä/	father	/ŏ/	pot	/o͞o/	boot
/ĕ/	pet	/ō/	go	/ŭ/	cut
/ē/	be	/ô/	paw, for	/û/	turn, circle
				/yo͞o/	use

/ə/ about, silent, pencil, lemon, circus

This pronunciation key is adapted from *The American Heritage School Dictionary*, published by American Heritage Publishing Co., Inc., and Houghton Mifflin Company.

A

a·ca·cia (ə kā′shə) A kind of tree with yellow flowers and feathery leaves that grows mainly in warm places.

ac·com·pa·ny (ə kŭm′pə nē) To be with or go along with.

ad·just (ə jŭst′) 1. To change so as to be more comfortable or correct. 2. To become suited and used to where one lives.

ad·mi·ra·tion (ăd mə rā′shən) Very great respect.

a·dor·a·ble (ə dôr′ə bəl) Very charming or cute.

af·ford (ə fôrd′) To be able to spare or pay for.

air·shaft (âr′shăft) A walled-in open space down through the middle of a building to let in air.

an·cient (ān′shənt) Very old.

an·es·thet·ic (ăn ĭs thĕt′ĭk) A drug or gas given to a patient before an operation to keep the patient from feeling pain.

an·noy (ə noi′) To bother or disturb.

ap·point·ment (ə point′mənt) An arrangement to meet at a certain time and place.

ap·proach (ə prōch′) To come near to.

ap·prove (ə proōv′) 1. To agree to. 2. To think well of.

a·ri·a (är′ē ə) A piece of music for a solo singer.

as·ton·ish (ə stŏn′ĭsh) To surprise or amaze.

as·tron·o·mer (ə strŏn′ə mər) A scientist who studies the planets, stars, and so forth.

as·tron·o·my (ə strŏn′ə mē) The study of the universe beyond the earth, such as stars, planets, and comets.

at·tach (ə tăch′) To join together or fasten.

a·ware (ə wâr′) Knowing about: *He's aware of his mistake.*

awe (ô) A feeling of great wonder or respect.

B

bab·ble (băb′əl) 1. Continuing speechlike sounds that the hearer cannot understand. 2. To make such sounds.

ă pat / ā pay / â care / ä father / ĕ pet / ē be / ĭ pit / ī pie / î fierce / ŏ pot / ō go
ô paw, for / oi noise / o͝o book / o͞o boot / ou out / ŭ cut / û turn / th thin / *th* this
hw which / zh pleasure / ə about, silent, pencil, lemon, circus

bean curd (bēn kûrd) A food often used in Chinese and Japanese cooking that is made from soybeans and looks somewhat like cheese.

beech (bēch) A kind of nut tree.

be·hold (bǐ hōld') To see.

bel·low (bĕl'ō) To make a loud roaring noise.

bleach·ers (blē'chərz) Uncovered bench seats for people watching outdoor sports.

blend (blĕnd) 1. To mix together. 2. To appear to be the same color: *A chameleon blends with the leaf it is sitting on.*

bluff[1] (blŭf) To fool or mislead someone: *He pretended that he wasn't afraid, but he was really bluffing.*

bluff[2] (blŭf) A high, steep cliff.

bolt (bōlt) 1. A sliding metal bar used to fasten a door or gate. 2. To lock with a bolt.

bom·bard (bŏm bärd') To shower someone else with repeated talking: *After the meeting, the reporters bombarded the mayor with questions.*

bra·vo (brä'vō) A word used to show enjoyment of someone's performance.

but·ter·fly valve (bŭt'ər flī vălv) The part of a car's engine that controls the flow of air between the air filter and the carburetor. It is so called because it looks somewhat like a butterfly's wings when in motion.

C

calm (käm) Not excited; quiet.

ca·noe (kə nōō') A light, slim boat that is moved by paddling.

ca·per (kā'pər) A playful jump or hop. —**cut capers.** To jump around playfully.

car·bu·re·tor (kär'bə rā tər) The part of the car where gasoline and air are mixed.

ca·reer (kə rîr') A job that one might make a life's work: *She went to law school because she wanted a career as a lawyer.*

cell (sĕl) The smallest part of a living substance (*blood cell, brain cell*): *A single cell is so tiny that you cannot see it unless you are looking into a microscope.*

cel·lo (chĕl'ō) A string musical instrument that looks like a large violin.

chap·let (chăp′lĭt) A circle made of flowers, leaves, or berries that is worn on the head for decoration.

chro·nom·e·ter (krə nŏm′ĭ tər) A very exact clock often used in astronomy or science experiments.

co·bra (kō′brə) A poisonous snake that lives in Africa and Asia.

com·et (kŏm′ĭt) A heavenly object that travels around the sun and looks like a fireball with a long tail. A comet is actually made up of frozen material, and the sun's light and heat make it look bright.

com·pli·ment (kŏm′plə mənt) 1. To say something nice to or about someone. 2. A statement praising someone.

com·pos·er (kəm pō′zər) A person who writes music.

con·cerned (kən sûrnd′) 1. Worried. 2. Interested or a part of: *As far as I'm concerned, the plans for the picnic sound fine.*

con·cert (kŏn′sûrt) A performance of music.

con·fi·dence (kŏn′fĭ dəns) Trust or faith: *He had a lot of confidence in his doctor.*

con·fi·den·tial (kŏn fĭ dĕn′shəl) Told in secret.

con·stant (kŏn′stənt) Happening over and over again.

con·stel·la·tion (kŏn stə lā′shən) A group of stars that is named for the animal, object, or storybook character that it is said to look like: *the Big Dipper; Orion the Hunter; the Great Bear.*

con·stit·u·ent (kən stĭch′o͞o ənt) A person represented by an elected leader: *State governors must think of all their constituents.*

con·ven·ient (kən vēn′yənt) Easy to reach.

coun·cil (koun′səl) A group of people called together to give advice and solve problems.

cre·ate (krē āt′) To make.

curd (kûrd) See **bean curd.**

ă pat / ā pay / â care / ä father / ĕ pet / ē be / ĭ pit / ī pie / î fierce / ŏ pot / ō go
ô paw, for / oi noise / o͝o book / o͞o boot / ou out / ŭ cut / û turn / th thin / *th* this
hw which / zh pleasure / ə about, silent, pencil, lemon, circus

D

daw·dle (dôd′l) To move more slowly than necessary.

de·coy (dē′koi) An object used to trick a person or an animal: *A wooden duck placed on a lake to attract live ducks is a decoy.*

de·lude (dĭ lōōd′) To mislead or trick.

de·mand (dĭ mănd′) To ask in a forceful way.

de·ny (dĭ nī′) To declare that something is untrue.

de·sign (dĭ zīn′) 1. To invent or plan a pattern of lines or colors. 2. A plan, drawing, or pattern.

des·per·ate (dĕs′pər ĭt) Willing to do almost anything because of having a problem that seems hopeless.

dis·gust·ed (dĭs gŭs′tĭd) Very angry or annoyed.

dis·tant (dĭs′tənt) Far away or far apart.

dis·tem·per (dĭs tĕm′pər) A very serious animal disease.

dis·tinct (dĭ stĭngkt′) 1. Unlike; different from others. 2. Clear; easily seen or heard.

du·et (dōō ĕt′) A musical piece performed by two people.

E

earth·en·ware (ûr′thən wâr) Made of clay that has been hardened by heat: *We ate soup from earthenware bowls.*

el·e·gant (ĕl′ĭ gənt) Very tasteful; nicer than the ordinary: *The furniture in that room was so elegant that I was almost afraid to sit on it.*

el·e·vat·ed (ĕl′ə vā tĭd) 1. Lifted up. 2. A train that runs on tracks built over a street.

em·brace (ĕm brās′) To hug.

en·chant·er (ĕn chănt′ər) A person in a story who can cast spells and perform magic.

en·vy (ĕn′vē) 1. A feeling of unhappiness because of someone else's good fortune. 2. A person or object that brings on such a feeling: *Her good looks were the envy of all her friends.* 3. To wish for what is someone else's: *We all envy Jane's success.*

ex·pres·sion (ĭk sprĕsh′ən) 1. A look that shows a certain feeling: *He had an angry expression on his face.* 2. A particular saying: *"Keep your chin up" is a well-known expression.*

F

fa·bled (fā′bəld) Well known in stories but perhaps not real.

fac·tu·al (făk′choo əl) True.

fame (fām) The state of being well known and admired.

fang (făng) A long, sharp tooth.

fil·ter (fĭl′tər) An object through which liquid or air can pass to become cleaned.

flab·ber·gast (flăb′ər găst) To amaze or astonish by doing or saying something completely unexpected.

flat·ter[1] (flăt′ər) More flat.

flat·ter[2] (flăt′ər) To say pleasing things to someone in order to get something.

for·eign·er (fôr′ə nər) A person from another country.

frac·tured (frăk′chərd) Broken.

frail (frāl) Not having a strong body; weak.

frank·ness (frăngk′nəs) A truthful way of speaking; honesty.

frol·ic (frŏl′ĭk) To play.

G

gar·land (gär′lənd) A chain of flowers worn as a necklace or headpiece.

ghee (gē) A type of butter used in India and neighboring countries.

gnarled (närld) Having knots and being no longer smooth: *People who do certain types of work with their hands all their lives are likely to have gnarled fingers when they grow old.*

gra·cious·ness (grā′shəs nəs) Kindness; charm.

grim (grĭm) Not pleased; not happy; stern.

grip (grĭp) 1. A tight hold. 2. To hold tightly.

groom (groom) 1. A man just married or about to be married. 2. A person who takes care of horses. 3. To clean and brush horses.

gust (gŭst) A strong, sudden burst of wind: *That quick gust blew my hat off my head.*

H

haunch (hônch) The hip and upper leg of an animal.

ă pat / ā pay / â care / ä father / ĕ pet / ē be / ĭ pit / ī pie / î fierce / ŏ pot / ō go
ô paw, for / oi noise / o͝o book / o͞o boot / ou out / ŭ cut / û turn / th thin / *th* this
hw which / zh pleasure / ə about, silent, pencil, lemon, circus

hes·i·tate (hĕz′ĭ tāt) 1. To pause. 2. To be slow to decide or uncertain.

hoarse (hôrs) Rough-sounding or husky.

hob·ble (hŏb′əl) To walk with a limp.

ho·gan (hō′gən) An earth-covered Navajo home.

hon·ey·suck·le (hŭn′ē sŭk əl) A type of vine with sweet-smelling flowers.

hor·ri·fy (hôr′ə fī) To shock or frighten terribly.

hos·tile (hŏs′təl) 1. Unfriendly. 2. Having to do with an enemy.

hov·er (hŭv′ər) To stay in one place in the air by rapidly beating the wings: *The mosquito hovered over my bed.*

hud·dle (hŭd′l) 1. A closely crowded group. 2. To crowd closely together. 3. A short gathering together of football players to plan the next play.

hu·mil·i·at·ing (hyōō mĭl′ē āt ĭng) Very embarrassing.

hurl (hûrl) To throw with great force.

I

ig·nore (ĭg nôr′) To pay no attention to.

im·me·di·ate (ĭ mē′dē ĭt) Taking place at once.

im·pec·ca·ble (ĭm pĕk′ə bəl) Absolutely perfect.

im·pu·dent (ĭm′pyə dənt) Bold and often rude: *The child was punished for making an impudent remark to the adults.*

in·jec·tion (ĭn jĕk′shən) A shot.

in·quire (ĭn kwīr′) To ask.

in·sert¹ (ĭn sûrt′) To put in.

in·sert² (ĭn′sûrt) Something put in: *When he wrote the paper, he knew that he would have to add something later in the middle, so he left space for that insert.*

in·sult (ĭn sŭlt′) To do or say something that is unkind or makes another angry.

in·tent (ĭn tĕnt′) Purpose.

in·ter·rupt (ĭn tə rŭpt′) 1. To break in and start to speak while someone else is still talking. 2. To make something stop for a while: *The rain interrupted our game for an hour.*

in·tro·duce (ĭn trə dōōs′) 1. To present or show for the first time. 2. To bring together people who have never met before.

in·vis·i·ble (ĭn vĭz′ə bəl) Impossible to be seen.

in·volve (ĭn vŏlv′)　1. To bring into: *Don't involve me in your argument.*　2. To have as a necessary part: *Being a good ball player involves a lot of practice.*

J

jo·ta (hō′tä)　A lively Spanish dance.

jour·nal (jûr′nəl) A newspaper or magazine dealing with a particular subject: *The Medical Journal is read by doctors.*

L

lab·o·ra·to·ry (lăb′rə tôr ē)　A place where doctors or scientists work with experiments.

lank·y (lăng′kē)　Tall and thin.

larch (lärch)　A tree in the pine family.

lens (lĕnz)　A curved piece of glass that can bring faraway things into closer view: *The lens on that telescope was very powerful.*

loom (lōōm)　A frame on which yarn or thread is woven to make cloth.

lus·trous (lŭs′trəs)　Gleaming; shiny.

M

mag·nif·i·cent　(măg nĭf′ĭ sənt) Splendid; grand; outstanding.

ma·ha·ra·ja　(mä hə rä′jə)　In olden times, a prince or king of India.

ma·zur·ka (mə zûr′kə) 1. A lively Polish dance. 2. A piece of music written for this Polish dance.

me·lee (mā lā′)　A fight filled with confusion.

me·sa (mā′sə)　A hill with steep sides and a flat top.

min·gle (mĭng′gəl)　To become mixed or combined.

mock (mŏk)　To make fun of.

mod·est (mŏd′ĭst)　Not bragging about oneself: *When he was praised for his bravery in rescuing the drowning dog, he said modestly, "It was nothing."*

ă pat / ā pay / â care / ä father / ĕ pet / ē be / ĭ pit / ī pie / î fierce / ŏ pot / ō go
ô paw, for / oi noise / ŏŏ book / ōō boot / ou out / ŭ cut / û turn / th thin / *th* this
hw which / zh pleasure / ə about, silent, pencil, lemon, circus

moon gate (mo͞on gāt)   In a Chinese wall, an opening in the shape of a circle that is large enough for one to pass through.

mo·tion (mō′shən)   1. To make a signal, often with a hand. 2. A movement. 3. In club meetings, a suggestion that has to be voted on.

mud·dle (mŭd′l)   1. To get mixed up or confused. 2. A mess.

muf·fle (mŭf′əl)   1. To cover in order to keep warm. 2. To cover in order to make less noise.

N

nec·tar (nĕk′tər)   A sweet liquid in some flowers that bees use to make honey.

ne·on (nē′ŏn)   A colorless gas found in tiny amounts in the air. When charged with electricity, it gives off a colored glow. Therefore it is often encased in clear glass tubes and used for signs.

net[1] (nĕt)   1. A piece of loosely woven cloth that is often used to catch fish. 2. To catch in a net.

net[2] (nĕt)   To bring in a gain of: *We'll need to net at least three runs in the next two innings.*

O

ob·ser·va·to·ry (əb zûr′və tôr ē)   A place built to house a huge telescope used by astronomers.

ob·serve (əb zûrv′)   To notice; to watch carefully.

of·fi·cial (ə fĭsh′əl)   Chosen or appointed to a special job or task: *You are the official scorekeeper for the game.*

or·na·ment (ôr′nə mənt)   Something worn or used as a decoration.

ox·y·gen (ŏk′sĭ jən)   A gas that must be in the air in order for people and animals to breathe.

P

pace (pās)   1. The way or speed with which something happens: *We worked at a rapid pace.* 2. To walk back and forth across: *He was so nervous that he paced the floor.*

pad·dy (păd′ē)   A marshy or very wet field where rice is grown.

pang (păng)   A sudden, sharp feeling of pain, fear, or sadness.

pea·cock (pē′kŏk) A large, brightly colored bird that can spread its tail feathers out like a fan. Sometimes a person who is showing off is said to be "as proud as a peacock."

ped·dle (pĕd′l) To travel around selling something.

per·ish (pĕr′ĭsh) To die.

per·suade (pər swād′) To win over to one's way of thinking by reasoning or argument.

pe·ti·tion (pə tĭsh′ən) A written paper asking for something.

plump (plŭmp) Full; fleshy; rounded.

preen (prēn) To smooth down feathers with the beak.

pro·ceed (prō sēd′) To go onward.

pro·fes·sor (prə fĕs′ər) A teacher in a college.

prop (prŏp) To place a person or object so that it is leaning against something.

Q

qua·ver (kwā′vər) To shake or tremble.

queue (kyoo) 1. A line of people waiting for something. 2. A long pigtail.

R

ra·bies (rā′bēz) A deadly disease that people or animals can get from the bite of an infected animal.

ra·di·a·tor (rā′dē ā tər) 1. Something used to heat a room or building, often a set of pipes through which hot water or steam can move. 2. The part of a car that holds water to keep the engine from overheating.

rage (rāj) Very great anger.

razz (răz) *Slang.* To tease or make fun of.

re·cit·al (rĭ sīt′l) A musical performance, usually by one person.

reck·on (rĕk′ən) To think or suppose. **—reckoning.** The act of figuring something out: *According to my reckoning, we should be finished by five o'clock.*

ă pat / ā pay / â care / ä father / ĕ pet / ē be / ĭ pit / ī pie / î fierce / ŏ pot / ō go
ô paw, for / oi noise / oo book / oo boot / ou out / ŭ cut / û turn / th thin / *th* this
hw which / zh pleasure / ə about, silent, pencil, lemon, circus

re·frain (rĭ **frān'**) To keep oneself from doing something: *I try to refrain from eating too much candy.*

reins (rānz) 1. The straps that are attached to the bit in a horse's mouth and held by the rider to direct and control the horse. 2. **rein.** To pull in these straps to slow a horse down.

ren·der (**rĕn'**dər) To give or provide: *Our business will render prompt service to all who need it.*

rep·re·sent (rĕp rĭ **zĕnt'**) To act for; stand for: *The President represents the people of the United States.*

re·quest (rĭ **kwĕst'**) 1. To ask for politely. 2. Something asked for. 3. The act of asking for something.

res·o·nance (**rĕz'**ə nəns) A full, pleasing sound, especially that of a voice or musical instrument.

re·spect (rĭ **spĕkt'**) 1. To look up to; to think highly of. 2. To obey: *Respect your elders.* 3. A show of politeness: *He bowed respectfully to the audience.*

re·spec·tive (rĭ **spĕk'**tĭv) Having to do with two or more people or things: *The school bus dropped the children off at their respective homes.*

re·sult (rĭ **zŭlt'**) The way something turns out: *He got good results from his garden because he took good care of it.*

re·tire (rĭ **tīr'**) To stop working when one reaches a certain age.

re·volve (rĭ **vŏlv'**) To go around, especially in an orbit: *The moon revolves around the earth.*

rhythm (**rĭ***th***'**əm) 1. A regular repeating of a beat, as in music. 2. A pattern of beats as in poetry when read aloud.

romp (rŏmp) To run around playfully.

rou·tine (roo **tēn'**) The usual way that things are happening.

ru·mor (**roo'**mər) A report spread by word of mouth which may or may not be true.

rus·tle (**rŭs'**əl) 1. A soft, quick, whispering sound. 2. To make a soft whispering sound.

S

sa·ri (**sä'**rē) A gownlike garment worn by women in India.

scaf·fold·ing (skăf′əl dĭng)　A platform put up beside a building for workers to stand on while they are repairing or working on the building.

scent (sĕnt)　A smell.

scoun·drel (skoun′drəl)　A rogue; a wicked person.

scrab·ble (skrăb′əl)　To use one's hands to search hurriedly for something.

scroll (skrōl)　A paper or paper-like roll on which something is written: *In olden times, people wrote on scrolls because there were no books.*

scur·ry (skûr′ē)　To run about hurriedly.

sep·a·rate[1] (sĕp′ə rāt)　To take apart or keep apart.

sep·a·rate[2] (sĕp′ə rĭt)　Single; not together; by itself.

shaft (shăft)　A beam of light.

shan't (shănt)　Shall not.

shin·gle (shĭng′gəl)　1. A piece of wood used along with many other pieces to cover the outside of a building. 2. To put shingles on a building.

shrill (shrĭl)　High-pitched and rather loud: *A shrill voice is often annoying.*

sig·na·ture (sĭg′nə chər)　The name of a person as written by that person.

sin·is·ter (sĭn′ĭ stər)　Suggesting something fearsome: *The full moon made sinister shadows in the graveyard.*

sire (sīr)　1. A father. 2. When capitalized, a title of respect given a king.

skull (skŭl)　The bony framework of the head.

soar (sôr)　To fly high into the air.

so·lu·tion (sə lōō′shən)　1. A liquid mixture. 2. The answer to a problem or mystery.

so·na·ta (sə nä′tə)　A certain type of musical piece having several different parts.

soothe (sōō*th*)　To make calm or comfortable.

source (sôrs)　Where something comes from: *What is the source of that awful noise?*

sped (spĕd)　Did speed; went very fast.

ă pat / ā pay / â care / ä father / ĕ pet / ē be / ĭ pit / ī pie / î fierce / ŏ pot / ō go
ô paw, for / oi noise / ŏŏ book / ōō boot / ou out / ŭ cut / û turn / th thin / *th* this
hw which / zh pleasure / ə about, silent, pencil, lemon, circus

spinal cord (spī′nəl kôrd) The central nerve that runs inside the backbone from the brain and branches off below into smaller nerves.

spinney (spĭn′ē) A thicket of small bushes or trees.

sprang (sprăng) Jumped up.

sprig (sprĭg) A small twig of a plant.

ster·ile (stĕr′əl) Free from disease-causing germs.

strand (strănd) A single, string-like piece often with other pieces: *That rope has three strands twisted together.*

strut (strŭt) To walk in a show-off manner.

stun (stŭn) To surprise someone greatly.

stu·pen·dous (stoo pĕn′dəs) 1. Wonderful. 2. Amazingly large.

sub·way (sŭb′wā) An underground railroad system found in some large cities.

sur·face (sûr′fəs) The outside or top: *The surface of a body of water is where the water meets the air.*

sus·pect¹ (sə spĕkt′) To think, but to have no real proof, that someone did something.

sus·pect² (sŭs′pĕkt) A person who is thought to have committed a crime.

sus·pi·cious (sə spĭsh′əs) Tending not to believe or trust someone else.

T

tac·tics (tăk′tĭks) A plan of action to try to get something one wants.

tan·go (tăng′gō) A kind of Latin American dance.

task (tăsk) A job or duty.

tas·sel (tăs′əl) 1. A bunch of string or thread tied at one end and hanging free at the other, used as a decoration. 2. Something looking like this decoration, such as the group of flowers on a corn plant.

tel·e·scop·ic (tĕl ə skŏp′ĭk) Having to do with a telescope: *A telescopic star is a star that can only be seen through a telescope.*

tem·per·a·ment·al (tĕm prə-mĕn′tl) Easily angered or excited.

ten·ant (tĕn′ənt) A person who pays rent to live in a house, farm, or apartment owned by someone else.

thatch (thăch) 1. Straw or leaves used to make a roof. 2. To cover a house with straw or leaves.

thy (*thī*) In olden days, a word meaning *your*.

tim·id (tĭm′ĭd) Shy; easily frightened.

to·ken (tō′kən) A piece of metal used in place of money on buses, subway trains, and the like.

tor·rent (tôr′ənt) A very forceful, strong rain.

tra·di·tion·al (trə dĭsh′ən əl) Passed along in a particular family or country as part of a culture: *Having a turkey on Thanksgiving Day is traditional in many American families.*

tram·ple (trăm′pəl) To step heavily, causing damage to whatever is underfoot.

tre·men·dous (trĭ mĕn′dəs) Very large or loud.

tres·pass (trĕs′păs) To go onto someone else's property or anywhere one shouldn't be.

tri·al (trī′əl) A time in court for deciding whether or not a person is guilty of a crime. **—on trial.** In the process of being tried for a certain crime in court.

tri·pod (trī′pŏd) An object with three legs that holds something off the ground.

trudge (trŭj) To walk in a slow, heavy-footed manner.

turn·stile (tûrn′stīl) A post set in an entrance with arms coming out from the middle. To get through the entrance, a person drops a coin or token into a slot, and the arms turn to let the person go through.

tur·quoise (tûr′koiz) A blue-green mineral often used in making jewelry, ornaments, and belts.

U

un·a·ware (ŭn ə wâr′) Not knowing or realizing.

un·daunt·ed (ŭn dôn′tĭd) Not upset or discouraged because of what has happened.

ă pat / ā pay / â care / ä father / ĕ pet / ē be / ĭ pit / ī pie / î fierce / ŏ pot / ō go
ô paw, for / oi noise / o͝o book / o͞o boot / ou out / ŭ cut / û turn / th thin / *th* this
hw which / zh pleasure / ə about, silent, pencil, lemon, circus

V

valve (vălv) A movable part that controls the flow of a gas or liquid in a machine. See also **butterfly valve.**

vow (vou)   1. A very serious promise. 2. To make a serious promise.

W

waltz (wôlts) 1. A type of dance. 2. A piece of music, with three beats to the measure, that goes along with the dance.

warp (wôrp) 1. To bend or twist out of shape. 2. In weaving, the threads that run along the length of a piece of cloth and are crossed by the weft.

weft (wĕft)   In weaving, the crosswise threads that run between the warp threads. Also called **woof.**

wir·y (wīr′ē) Small and slim, but not necessarily weak.

wisp·y (wĭsp′ē) Thin and slight: *One man's beard was thick, but the other's was wispy.*

Artist Credits

Illustrators: PP. 9–18, GERALD MCDERMOTT; P. 19, ATI FORBERG; PP. 20–37, LOIS EHLERT; PP. 38–39, DOROTHEA SIERRA; PP. 41–45, JOHN HAM; PP. 46–56, DAVID MCPHAIL; P. 57, GEOFFREY HODGKINSON; PP. 68–92, DEL NICHOLS; P. 93, BRUCE COCHRAN; PP. 94–98, JOHN HAM; P. 99, DAVID MCPHAIL; PP. 100–109, ERNEST H. SHEPARD; PP. 113–135, JOHN MC-INTOSH; PP. 136–142, JOYCE WINKLE, designer; PP. 143–147, JOHN HAM; P. 148, MARC BROWN; PP. 156–167, HERBERT DANSKA; PP. 170–179, JERRY PINKNEY; PP. 180–186, JOHN HAM; PP. 187–211, JEAN KING; PP. 212–213, SUE THOMPSON; PP. 214–223, DON FREEMAN; PP. 227–246, MARGARET HATHAWAY; PP. 247–250, JOHN HAM; PP. 251–262, LYLE MILLER; P. 263, JARED D. LEE; PP. 264–265, SAS COLBY; PP. 266–281, DEE ANNE DYKE; PP. 282–299, CHRISTINE CZERNOTA; PP. 300–306, CALVIN BURNETT; P. 307, AL HIRSCHFELD drawing from The Margo Feiden Galleries, New York City; PP. 309–313, JOHN HAM; PP. 314–315, JEANETTE KEHL; PP. 316–335, CALVIN BURNETT; PP. 336–351, LEONARD LUBIN.

Photographers: P. 40, CHRISTIAN DELBERT; PP. 58–67, ERIK ANDERSON, PP. 136, 138–141, 142, CULVER PICTURES, INC.; P. 137, GEORGE MARTIN (DPI); P. 142, WIDE WORLD; P. 147, UNITED FRUIT COMPANY; PP. 149–155, JIM JACKSON; PP. 168–169, WESTERN WAYS FEATURES; PP. 282–299, BILL SUMNER; P. 308, ROBERT SWEDROE.

Book cover, title page, and magazine covers by DOROTHEA SIERRA.